# FASHION REBELS

# FASHION
# REBELS

## Style Icons Who Changed the World through Fashion

Carlyn Cerniglia Beccia

**ALADDIN**
New York London Toronto Sydney New Delhi

BEYOND WORDS
Hillsboro, Oregon

*To Charlotte—my fearless fashion rebel, and all the girls who dare to be different*

ALADDIN
An imprint of Simon & Schuster
Children's Publishing Division
1230 Avenue of the Americas
New York, NY 10020

BEYOND WORDS
20827 N.W. Cornell Road, Suite 500
Hillsboro, Oregon 97124-9808
503-531-8700 / 503-531-8773 fax
www.beyondword.com

This Beyond Words/Aladdin edition September 2016
Text and cover and interior illustrations copyright © 2016 by Carlyn Beccia
Cover copyright © 2016 by Beyond Words/Simon & Schuster, Inc.

Managing Editor: Lindsay S. Easterbrooks-Brown
Editors: Leah Brown, Nicole Geiger
Copyeditor: Jenefer Angell
Interior and cover design: Sara E. Blum
The text of this book was set in Fairfield LT Std.

For information about special discounts for bulk purchases, please contact
Simon & Schuster Special Sales at 1-866-506-1949 or business@simonandschuster.com.

The Simon & Schuster Speakers Bureau can bring authors to your live event.
For more information or to book an event contact the Simon & Schuster Speakers
Bureau at 1-866-248-3049 or visit our website at www.simonspeakers.com.

Manufactured in China 0616 SCP

10 9 8 7 6 5 4 3 2 1

Library of Congress Cataloging-in-Publication Data

Names: Beccia, Carlyn.
Title: Fashion rebels : style icons who changed the world through fashion /
Carlyn Cerniglia Beccia.
Description: Hillsboro, Orgeon : Beyond Words, New York : Aladdin, [2016] |
Includes bibliographical references.
Identifiers: LCCN 2015041456 (print) | LCCN 2016005287 (ebook) |
ISBN 9781582704883 (hardcover) | ISBN 9781582704876 (pbk.) | ISBN 9781481416818 (eBook)
Subjects: LCSH: Women's clothing—History. | Fashion—History. |
Women—Biography. | Celebrities—Biography.
Classification: LCC GT1720 .B435 2016 (print) | LCC GT1720 (ebook) | DDC
391/.2—dc23
LC record available at http://lccn.loc.gov/2015041456

# CONTENTS

# WHY FASHION MATTERS

*If you put something on and it doesn't look good,*
*the fashion police aren't going to come and take you away.*
*And if they do, you might have some fun in jail.*

IRIS APFEL, NONAGENARIAN FASHION GURU

Today, we take for granted that Lady Gaga can wear slabs of meat or Kermit the Frogs affixed to her skin and call it a dress. Sure, she will get her share of weird looks, but no one is going to lock her up for being different and many will respect her more for making a statement. (The frog dress was a statement against wearing furs and the meat dress was to support gay rights in the military.) Such was not the case for many of the women in this book. Not only would wearing meat as a dress have been frowned upon, most could not even wear pants. And if they did . . . well, Joan of Arc got in a heap load of trouble for that one (page 66).

Despite often limited choices, many women throughout history have refused to dress like everyone else. The reasons behind their style decisions were as varied as the women wearing them. Some used clothing to communicate power. Check out how England's Queen Elizabeth I (page 18) decorated her dresses with imagery of body parts to send the message that she was the boss. Some used fashion to express themselves and just have a little fun. No, Lady Gaga was not the first to make a fashion statement out of food. Entertainer Josephine Baker beat her to it by many decades (page 52). Some fashion rebels simply wanted more freedom of choice, such as when actress Katharine Hepburn pranced out of her dressing room nearly naked (page 60). And yes, some of these ladies are still changing fashion. It's anyone's guess how Madonna or Tavi Gavinson may reinvent herself next.

So why should we read their stories? Why does style matter? Fashion icon and entrepreneur Iris Apfel—born in 1921 and still killing it in the fashion world—probably knows the answer better than anyone. She says, "When you don't dress like everybody else, you don't have to think like everybody else."[1] The women in this book thought differently. They were confident, unique, fun, intelligent, and they didn't just change the world of fashion. They used fashion to change the world.

To help prepare you to be daring and different, you might first need some style inspiration. Take the quiz on the following page to see which icon's approach to fashion is the most natural starting point for you to find your own unique style.

# WHO IS YOUR STYLE ICON?

**Pick Your Favorite shoe:**
1. Converse
2. Classic black flats
3. Embroidered slipper
4. Gladiator sandals
5. High heels
6. A red "statement" shoe

**Choose Your Favorite color:**
1. Orange
2. Pink
3. Baby blue
4. Gold
5. White
6. Red

**My go-to accessory to feel pretty is:**
1. Funky socks
2. A tiara
3. A lace shawl
4. A gold statement necklace
5. A fake fur stole
6. An animal-print scarf

**Pick Your Favorite flower:**
1. I prefer edible arrangements—they are flowers you can eat!
2. Lily of the valley
3. Violet
4. Lotus
5. Rose
6. Orchid

**I want my clothes to:**
1. Allow me to move freely
2. Be girly and sweet
3. Make me feel regal
4. Make me feel powerful
5. Be fun, playful, and make a few heads turn
6. Be exotic and totally unique

**I am the most comfortable when I am:**
1. Busting a move on the dance floor
2. Hanging out with girlfriends
3. On a horse
4. Getting people to do my bidding

5. Smiling for the camera
6. Shocking people

**If one word could define my style it would be:**
1. Relaxed
2. Classic
3. Dazzling
4. Dynamic
5. Flirtatious
6. Audacious

**If I could visit one city it would be:**
1. Chicago
2. New York
3. Vienna, Austria
4. Cairo, Egypt
5. Los Angeles
6. Paris, France

**If I was a different creature I would be a:**
1. Platypus
2. Blue jay
3. Poodle
4. Cobra
5. Kitten
6. Jaguar

**I would most like to study:**
1. Psychology. I want to know what makes people tick.
2. Cooking. I love to take care of people.
3. Economics. Money is power.
4. Social Studies. I plan to be president someday.
5. Liberal Arts. I want to learn everything.
6. Art. I want to inspire others.

**I feel pretty because:**

1. "True beauty is not related to what color your hair is or what color your eyes are. True beauty is about who you are as a human being, your principles, your moral compass."[2]
2. "Elegance is the only beauty that never fades."[3]
3. "Courage! I have shown it for years."[4]
4. "I will not be triumphed over."[5]
5. "We are all of us stars, and we deserve to twinkle."[6]
6. "I'm not intimidated by anyone. Everyone is made with two arms, two legs, a stomach and a head."[7]

## RESULTS

**Count up all your 1s, 2s, 3s, 4s, 5s, and 6s.**

### You have mostly 1s

**Your style icon is Ellen DeGeneres.** You are that cool girl that everyone wants to be friends with because your style is totally effortless. Fashion isn't high up on your list of priorities and you probably got bored taking this quiz. You have better things to do—like charming the world.

### You have mostly 2s

**The iconic lovely that appeals to you most is Audrey Hepburn.** Your style is classic, ladylike, and you never have to worry about looking back at a picture and saying, "I can't believe I wore *that*!" Even in Keds and a crisp white blouse, you look one hundred percent pulled together. You are naturally upbeat and choose fashions that make you feel lighthearted.

### You have mostly 3s

**You look to the bold Marie Antoinette for inspiration.** Congratulations, Princess. You go all out when it comes to fashion and probably have the tallest hair in the room. And why not? You are royalty and deserve to get the attention.

### You have mostly 4s

**You're drawn to the daring styles of Cleopatra.** No one better mess with you, especially when you have your pet snake wrapped around your stylish body. You are a power dresser, but have a feminine side too. People often mistake you for a Greek goddess, and you are the first to be voted "most likely to succeed." It's tough being so darn alluring.

### You have mostly 5s

**You love the glam fashions of Marilyn Monroe.** Your complex style lets you slam-dunk during gym class, even while wearing diamonds. You may practice your air kiss in front of the mirror to have a little fun, but you also know when to hit the books.

### You have mostly 6s

**You're most influenced by the fashionista Josephine Baker.** You are the life of the party and the first to get on the dance floor. You like to make people laugh, but you will never let them laugh at you. You are most comfortable in bold styles—anything that matches your fear-less fashion sense, from animal-print tights to red enamel bangles.

Make a
Grand
Entrance

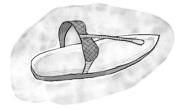

# CLEOPATRA VII
## 69 BCE–30 BCE

*Her beauty was not of itself absolutely without parallel,*
*not the kind to astonish those who saw her; but her presence*
*exerted an inevitable fascination.*

PLUTARCH DESCRIBING CLEOPATRA

In 48 BCE, Queen Cleopatra VII, Philopator of Egypt, was seriously down on her luck. Her father Ptolemy XII had died three years earlier. The River Nile, which Egyptians depended on to water crops, had failed to flood, causing famine throughout Egypt. The royal coffers were empty after years of overspending. (Keeping pet elephants with gold slippers will do that.)[1] And, oh, her brother was trying to kill her.

Cleopatra fled the royal palace in Alexandria and went south to Arabia (a region that today is several different countries, such as Kuwait, Saudi Arabia, and includes parts of Iraq).

Her Macedonian (Greek) family, the Ptolemies (pronounced tall-lom-mees), had ruled Egypt for nearly three hundred years. Before his death, her father had decreed that his eighteen-year-old daughter, Cleopatra VII, and her ten-year-old brother, Ptolemy XIII, would rule Egypt together. Her brother had other ideas. He had no intention of sharing his crown.[2] No, it would be far easier to get rid of big sis and rule alone. But Cleopatra was not about to be pushed out without a fight. So with the desert winds threatening to whip the white ribbon diadem (the sacred crown of an Egyptian queen) off her head, Cleopatra planned to win back her rightful place on the throne. She needed to stage the comeback of a lifetime. She needed to make an unforgettable entrance.

Fortune was on her side when the powerful Roman General Julius Caesar landed off the coast of Alexandria to collect on an old debt owed by her father.[3] Cleopatra's only hope of getting Caesar to support her side was a private audience with him. Only one problem: her brother's army had Caesar's quarters surrounded. If Cleopatra was discovered putting one jeweled sandal into Caesar's quarters, baby brother would have her killed quicker than you can say khopesh (a curved sword Egyptians used to cut down enemies). She needed a disguise.

Legend has it that she had her small frame rolled up in a carpet (or laundry bag, depending on the translation) secured with a leather strap.[4] Other historians believe that she merely veiled her face, arguing that a queen of Egypt would never do something so undignified. Whether carpet or cloth hid her, she managed to smuggle herself into Caesar's quarters unnoticed.

The meeting was a dangerous gamble. Caesar could have called for Cleopatra's execution. It certainly would have been a quick and easy way to end the sibling rivalry. Historians still don't know what exactly Caesar thought of Cleopatra's grand entrance, but the next day, Caesar and Cleopatra were best buddies. From that day forward, Caesar supported Cleopatra's claim to the throne.[5]

Was it her beauty that charmed Caesar? Throughout history, Hollywood has portrayed Cleopatra as a gorgeous, exotic temptress in gauzy veils, dripping in jewels. The jewels part is accurate. Cleopatra wore enough pearls, gems, and gold to practically sink the royal barge.[6] The looks part . . . that is still up for debate. The truth is no one knows for sure what Cleopatra looked like. Coins that she commissioned to celebrate

her reign are not exactly flattering. Sure, she looks stylish. Her hair is in the Roman fashion with elaborate braids knotted in the back and encircled by a diadem. But it's her facial features that are the most striking—bulging eyes, hooked nose, jutting chin, thick neck, and, on many coins, one curious Adam's apple.

Many historians have argued that Cleopatra's main objective with her coins was to look like a strong ruler. At the time, Egypt was in constant fear of invasion from Rome. And Roman women never held public office or voted, and they certainly would never rule. Perhaps the only way Cleopatra could communicate her strength was to look like the only type of leader Romans believed possessed strength—a man.

Written accounts of her appearance are not particularly flattering either. The Roman historian Plutarch described her beauty as "not the kind to astonish those who saw her."[7] Plutarch did say that she had "persuasive charm" and compared her voice to a "many-stringed instrument," but that's not exactly waxing poetic.[8] Most likely, Cleopatra's mind was also as varied as a "many-stringed instrument." Historians believe she spoke between seven and nine languages and wrote treatises on astronomy.[9] Caesar was probably fascinated by her wit, intelligence, and, most importantly, her ambition. (They shared that last trait.)

For a time Caesar and Cleopatra lived happily in Rome, but their union was not to last long. Only Cleopatra's ambition would endure. In 44 BCE, Caesar was assassinated by members of the Roman Senate and Cleopatra fled to Egypt with their young son. By 37 BCE, she formed a political and romantic alliance with Roman general Mark Antony to conquer Asia Minor and unify it with Egypt. Antony had the army and Cleopatra gave him her navy. But she needed the support of the Egyptian people to wage war. She also needed Egyptians to view her as a goddess and not as a money-hungry Greek tyrant. (Egyptians didn't care for foreigners—especially Greeks.) And what's the best way to create the right image? Well, fashion, of course!

Most Egyptian rulers wore a crown called a uraeus (pronounced yoo-ree-uhs) that was adorned with two rearing female cobras The uraeus was believed to protect the Egyptian pharaohs. Cleopatra adopted the crown too, but instead of two cobras, hers had three.[10]

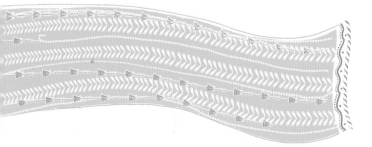

She also started dressing in the colorful robes of Isis, the goddess of motherhood, fertility, and magic. She even went so far as to claim she was Isis reincarnated. How could you possibly lose a war with magic and three fierce snakes on your side?

Unfortunately, lose she did. At the Battle of Actium in 31 BCE, Antony's fleet surrendered to the Roman general Octavian, and Antony and Cleopatra fled back to Egypt. Cleopatra was ruined and had little hope of keeping her throne. Still, she wasn't about to be captured and paraded down the streets of Rome in chains like some prisoner of war. Legend has it she had an Egyptian cobra, or asp, smuggled into the palace in a basket of figs. Then she dressed in her royal robes, lay down on a golden sofa, and let the serpent bite her, thereby ending her dramatic life.

Despite her tragic end, Cleopatra's influence on the public imagination has continued for two thousand years, inspiring Hollywood movies, endless novels, and one of Shakespeare's most famous plays. Her goddess style can be seen in everything from statement choker necklaces, gold bangles, gladiator shoes, braided hair, white flowing gowns, and the always beguiling "cat eye" lined eyes. Cleopatra knew not only how to make a grand entrance, but one enduring grand exit.

Cleopatra most likely had a strong nose, honey colored skin that she whitened with lead makeup, and deep-set eyes. Sometimes she had gold dust sprinkled on her hair and eyebrows.

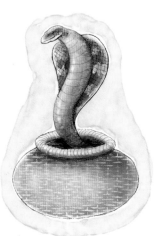

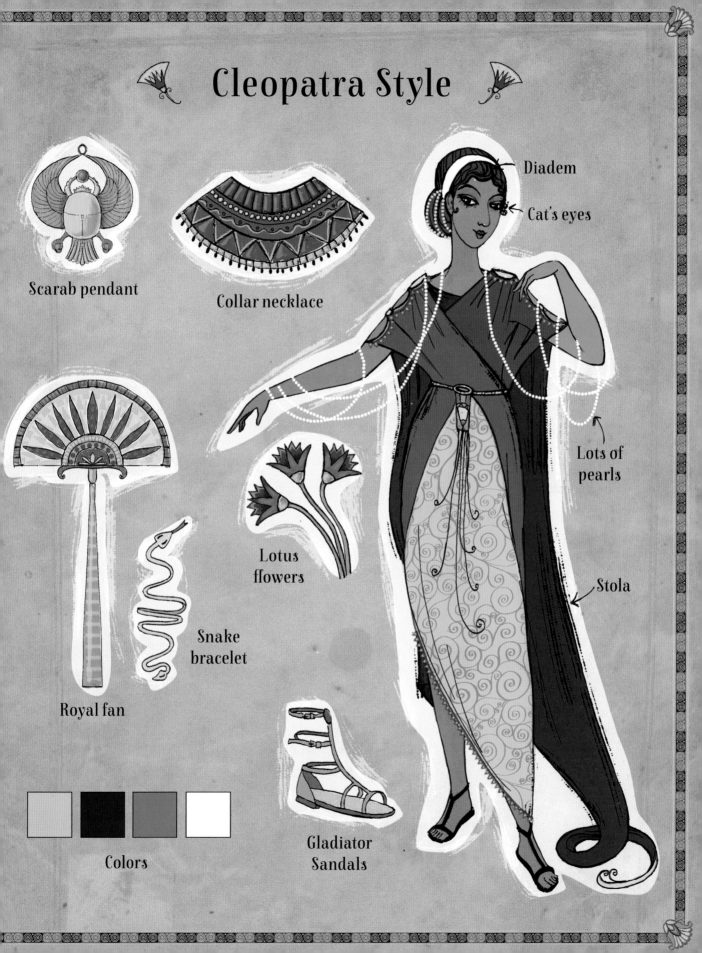

# Cleopatra Style

Scarab pendant

Collar necklace

Diadem

Cat's eyes

Royal fan

Snake bracelet

Lotus fflowers

Lots of pearls

Stola

Gladiator Sandals

Colors

# All Eyes on the Queen

# ELIZABETH I
## 1533–1603

*I will have but one mistress here and no master!*

ELIZABETH I

At the ripe old age of eight, Princess Elizabeth of England, daughter of King Henry VIII (he of the many wives) declared to her good friend Robert Dudley, "I will never marry."[1] She had good cause; both her mother, Anne Boleyn, and her stepmother, Kathryn Howard had lost their heads as a result of their marriages to the king. One could hardly fault Elizabeth for associating marriage with becoming a head shorter. Of course, no one believed an eight-year-old would know what her future held for her. But they should have. Elizabeth really meant it.

This defiance created a serious problem twenty years later when Elizabeth became queen. You see, royalty in Elizabeth's day *had* to marry because it secured political alliances between nations, thereby protecting them from invasion. Plus, women were far too weak and addled to rule. Or so everyone believed.[2]

Elizabeth was having none of this whole marriage business. Instead, she declared she would marry England. But, it is not enough to just say something. You have to dress the part too. Throughout her reign, Elizabeth used fashion to show she was fully capable of ruling—alone.

This wasn't the easiest task. In the fifteenth century, men were the fashion plates, not women. When her father Henry VIII ruled England, fabrics on women's dresses were certainly rich, but the shape was a simple square neck dress over a white undergarment called a kirtle. The men at court had far more fun. They wore fancy bejeweled doublets (a short jacket) with enormous padding in the shoulders and colorful hose that showed off their legs. These hose didn't cover one's private parts (underwear had not been invented yet) so men wore padded pouches called codpieces to conceal themselves. Codpieces got larger and larger until eventually it was the first thing that entered a room.

Elizabeth had enough of the boys getting all the attention. When she became queen, Elizabeth made sure women's fashion took center stage and her style became more and more ostentatious. The sleeves of her dresses puffed out with padding and her skirts jutted out with the help of a wooden hoop called a farthingale. She wore enormous ruffs and veils that spread out around her head like the wings of a butterfly. Her clothing had enough bling to blind a person: dresses woven with threads of gold, endless pearls, diamond-encrusted bodices, gems in her hair, and embroidered gloves. Not content with a mediocre crown, she used padding in her hair and feathered plumes to create height.

If a dress had significance, she would commission a painting with her wearing the dress. In one royal portrait, she wore a dress decorated with eyes and ears. The message: Elizabeth could hear and see everything, so you better not try to double cross her. And as far as codpieces went, Elizabeth did not approve of them so they got smaller and smaller until they disappeared altogether.

Of course, just like high fashion today, not everyone had the means to dress like a queen. They sure did try, though. Courtiers who wanted to win Elizabeth's favor wore dresses with cinched waists and large sleeves to emulate the queen's preferred style.[3] Even the men tried to copy the queen, wearing corsets to cinch their waists and dyeing their beards red to match the queen's carrot-top hair.

Eventually, Elizabeth had 2,000 dresses, 628 jewels, too many gloves to count, and over 80 wigs (She lost her hair later in life).[4] One might get the impression that she spent a small fortune on fashion. In fact, Elizabeth's wardrobe expenses during the last four years of her reign were one-twelfth of her successor, James I.[5] Nope, instead of spending a fortune on her wardrobe, Elizabeth got her admirers to spend a fortune on her wardrobe. Anyone who wanted to win the queen's favor was expected to give Elizabeth the appropriate fashionable gift.[6] Fashion was a way to show your respect for the queen.

Although Elizabeth loved pretty things, fashion was never just about looking pretty. Everything Elizabeth wore was part of her larger political strategy to create the image of the "Virgin Queen" who was married only to England. Because white was the color of purity, she covered her face in white lead makeup and wore mostly white and black dresses. She drowned herself in white pearls—another symbol of her virtue. As one of her emblems, she adopted the white rose—the symbol of the Virgin Mary. And when she was being pestered by her council to marry, she had portraits of herself created with her hair long and loose. In the fifteenth century only an unmarried woman wore her hair down.

As you can see, Elizabeth was no fool. By convincing her people she was married to her country and not to a man, it gave her the power to rule alone. And guess what? She did a great job. Her strategy worked. Wearing a silver breastplate and white plumes in her hair, she

Elizabeth commissioned portraits of herself with an ermine. According to legend, the ermine represented purity because it would rather die than soil its white coat.

In Elizabeth's day, smallpox was a deadly disease that killed most people. Elizabeth contracted smallpox in the early part of her reign and it left her face scared. Her heavy, white lead makeup covered these smallpox scars.

rallied her troops and saw them defeat the Spanish in 1588. Through cunning statecraft, she kept England out of war for most of her reign, which allowed literacy, arts, science, and overseas explorations to flourish. She supported some of the most brilliant minds of her time, including playwright William Shakespeare, philosopher and scientist Sir Francis Bacon, and explorer Sir Walter Raleigh. At the beginning of Elizabeth's reign, England was broke, fighting over religion, and had no naval power. When she died in 1603, England had become a superpower and enjoyed a golden era of peace and prosperity.

Elizabeth accomplished all of this because she was a master of style as well as politics. Her fashion choices were similar to today's political advertisements and commercials as a means to promote (or push) a political message. In the end, Elizabeth's shrewdness allowed her sole ownership of both her body and her kingdom.

Before Elizabeth I lost her hair, she dyed it with rhubarb juice and oil of vitriol. Oil of vitriol, now known as sulfuric acid, is a caustic substance that caused hair loss. Elizabeth's white make up also contained lead, which caused her hairline to recede. Because so many women used lead makeup, a high forehead became *en vogue*.[8]

*"I know I have the body but of a weak and feeble woman, but I have the heart and stomach of a king."*[7]

ELIZABETH'S SPEECH TO HER TROOPS AT TILBURY

BEFORE DEFEATING THE SPANISH

# Elizabeth I Style

High-neck blouse

Pearls in hair

Red hair

White makeup

LEAD

Ruff

Pearl necklace

Embroidered top

Feathered fan

Embroidered gloves

Tudor rose

Colors

# Hair-Raising Fashion

# MARIE ANTOINETTE
## 1755–1793

*There is nothing new except what has been forgotten.*

ROSE BERTIN, MILLINER TO MARIE ANTOINETTE

No one dared touch a potato in eighteenth century France. They were dirty, lumpy, and caused leprosy.[1] Or so everyone feared—everyone except Marie Antoinette.

The potato's image makeover began with a simple party hosted by French chemist and pharmacist Antoine-Augustin Parmentier. Parmentier had concocted some delicious potato dishes and hoped to convince King Louis XVI and Queen Marie Antoinette to try them. After several bad wheat harvests, he saw the potato's potential to replace bread and feed France's starving population, if only he could get people to stop fearing it.

While Parmentier's cooks worked frantically, Marie Antoinette was busy with her coiffeur (hairdresser) creating a fabulous hairdo. The hairstyle was called the pouf and it wasn't exactly a simple wash-and-go look. Sometimes the pouf could take hours to create. First, Marie Antoinette's hair was teased by "frizzling" it with a hot iron. Then, horsehair cushions, wads of wool, or frames made from iron or wood were erected on top of her head. Over this structure, her real hair, along with human hair, horsehair, or yak hair was added. Then it was time for the real fun—the toppings. Marie Antoinette preferred white ostrich feathers, but ribbons, flowers, vegetables, and jewels could also work. To hold the hair in place, it was plastered with pomatum, a scented paste usually made from mutton suet and lard. Lastly, her hairdresser used a bellows-shaped object to blow a cloud of white

or gray powder over her head. With just a few hours of puffing, poufing, and powdering—*très bien*! Her hair sculpture was complete.[2]

Unfortunately, the pouf caused some difficulties. To start, it was really hard to walk around with hair as high as three feet.[3] Sometimes Marie Antoinette's hair was so tall that she was forced to stick her head out of her carriage like a dog or kneel on the carriage floor. Then, once she got to the ball, her head was sometimes too tall to fit through the doorway.[4] A few women copying the queen's pouf died when their hair got caught on lit chandeliers.[5] It certainly made for a fiery entrance.

On the day of the potato party, Marie Antoinette fortunately made it to Parmentier's party with her hair creation in one piece. Parmentier bowed to Louis and presented him with a bouquet of purple potato flowers. Louis immediately placed one delicate sprig in Marie Antoinette's

Marie Antoinette sometimes tied a ribbon or lace choker around her neck to complete the look.

pouf. The queen adored the look (along with the potato dishes). With Marie Antoinette as its supporter, the potato flower not only became the latest hair accessory, but the food itself became the hot new food delicacy.

Hair poufs were not the only way Marie Antoinette pushed fashion boundaries. Around 1780, she began wearing a loose, white dress called the gaulle. Instead of being fitted about the bodice like most dresses, the gaulle had thin layers of muslin loosely tied around the waist with a sash. (See illustration on following page). Most scandalous of all, it was worn without a corset—the standard undergarment worn to straighten the back and cinch the waist. Many critics accused Marie Antoinette of wearing only "underwear."[6] Soon lower-class women could easily copy Marie Antoinette's simple white dress. For the first time in France, fashion was no longer an indication of class. Even a maid could wear the same dress as a queen. Had Marie Antoinette pushed fashion boundaries too far? If she didn't look like a queen, would she still be treated like one?

Marie Antoinette wasn't worried. She spent hours locked away with her "Minister of Fashion," Rose Bertin, inventing colors for dresses, like "Paris Mud," the color of Paris' dirty streets.[7] "Cheveux de la Reine," was named after Marie Antoinette's golden hair. One grayish pink color named "Puce" became all the rage when Louis joked that it reminded him of fleas. (Puce is the French word for flea). Even more ridiculous, women rushed out to their dressmakers to get silk in "Caca de Dauphin"—a yellowish-brown color resembling the Dauphin (infant Prince) Louis Charles' first soiled diapers.[8]

As a fashion icon, Marie Antoinette continued to trend up. As a queen, her popularity plummeted. She spent hoards of money on fashions while a bad winter destroyed crops and the French economy tanked. As the people grew more hungry, Marie Antoinette realized her fashion choices needed to be more conservative so she reduced her expenses and wore simpler dresses without elaborate hair poufs. But it was too late. The public already blamed Marie Antoinette for the failed crops, and while the French upper class had enjoyed Parmentier's potato creations, the lower class was still suspicious of the potato and refused to accept it as a replacement for bread.

By 1789, a starving population reached its breaking point. The price of flour became too high for most people to afford bread. Over five thousand citizens stormed the palace at Versailles intent on making the extravagant queen pay for their misfortunes. Shouts of: "We have come for Queen's skin, so that we can make ribbons for our rosettes!" reverberated off the palace walls.[9] With only seconds to lose, Marie Antoinette escaped through a secret passage in her bedroom. When the furious mob broke through her door and found the queen had escaped, they slashed her bed and smashed her mirrors.

Many older ladies found the pouf ridiculous, which led to a hairstyle called La Grand Mère (the Grandmother), designed with special springs to lower the hair when a disapproving grandmother came around the corner.

Marie Antoinette, Louis, and their two children were later moved to Paris and confined in the Temple prison. Louis was found guilty of high treason and was sentenced to die by a new killing device—the guillotine. The guillotine was originally invented as a more humane method of enforcing the death penalty. Unfortunately, it made killing so quick and easy that wealthy aristocrats were marched off to slaughter like tomatoes put through a vegetable slicer. Louis had even helped with the original design, never thinking that someday it would be used on him.

On January 21, 1793, Marie Antoinette learned her husband was dead when she heard the drum roll outside her prison walls. On October 16, 1793, Marie Antoinette was also sentenced to die. Yet, even for her execution, she planned her outfit carefully. Behind the bars of her cell wall, she prepared her final fashion statement—a flowing dress in white, the color of a true fashion martyr. After her death, French women would wear similar loose, white dresses without corsets and a red ribbon around their necks to honor Marie Antoinette and all those who had lost their heads during the French Revolution. This simpler style eventually led to the less restricting empire-waist dress later worn by Empress Josephine Bonaparte, but it was Marie Antoinette who had set the fashion revolution in motion.

# MAKE A MARIE ANTOINETTE CHOKER

Chokers decorated with lace and ribbon became popular with Louis XV's famous courtier, Madame Pompadour. Marie Antoinette often wore chokers when she sat for her portraits. Here are the steps to make your own eighteenth-century-style choker.

### Supplies

- Thin ribbon
- Lace ribbon
- Fabric glue
- Charms, feathers, rhinestones, fabric flowers
- Measuring tape or ruler

---

### Step 1
Measure the circumference of your neck and cut the lace ribbon to that number.

### Step 2
Add approximately 15 inches to the circumference of your neck and cut the thinner ribbon to that number.
For example, if your neck is 10½ inches, cut the thin ribbon to 25½ inches.

### Step 3
Glue the thinner ribbon to the lace ribbon, making sure the ends overlap the lace ribbon evenly on both sides. To make it sturdier, you can also sew the ends. (Ask someone if you don't know how.)

### Step 4
Glue fabric flowers, bows, or rhinestones to the front. Wait for it to dry.

### Step 5
Tie the thinner ribbon into a bow at the back of your neck and prepare for the ball.

# Marie Antoinette Style

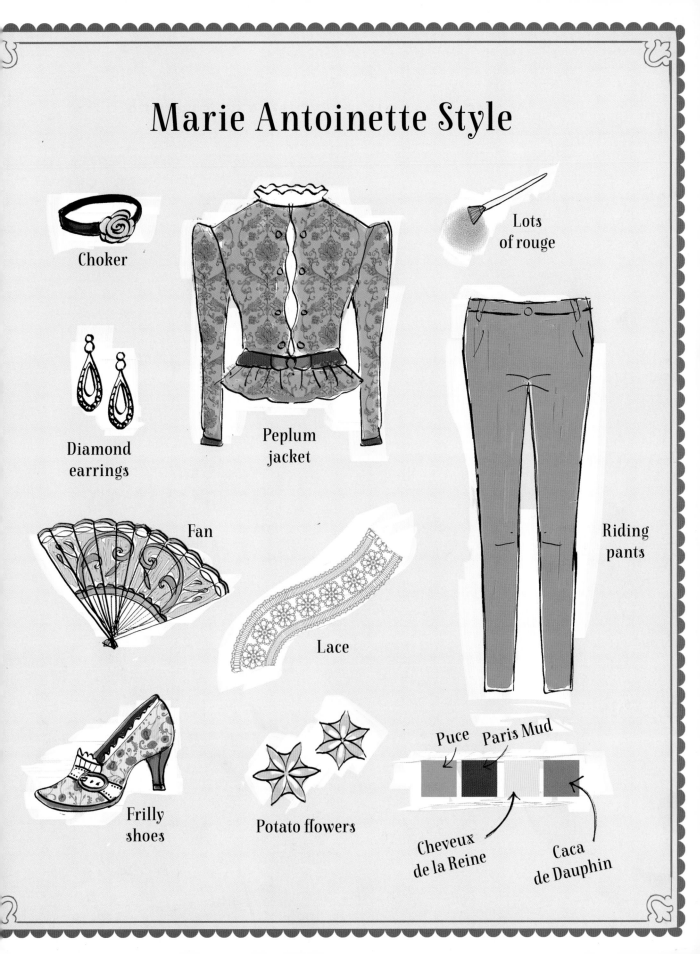

Choker

Lots of rouge

Diamond earrings

Peplum jacket

Fan

Lace

Riding pants

Frilly shoes

Potato fflowers

Puce

Paris Mud

Cheveux de la Reine

Caca de Dauphin

# The Hostess
of Fashion

# DOLLEY MADISON
## 1768–1849

*She could disarm envy itself.*

AN ADMIRER OF DOLLEY MADISON

On August 24, 1814, Dolley Madison stood on the roof of the White House turning her spyglass, hoping to see signs of an American victory. What she saw more than alarmed her. Through the clouds of dust and booming canons, carts filled with panicked men and women fled the city down Pennsylvania Avenue. Just days earlier, British forces had landed thirty-five miles north of the capital and had begun a slow march toward the White House. At this perilous point during the War of 1812, her husband, President James Madison, had left to join the ragtag American militia who were to defend the capital. Days earlier, he had instructed Dolley to leave the White House. Now with 4,000 British soldiers just a short distance away, time was running out.[1] She stuffed Madison's government papers into trunks and ordered they be placed into her carriage. Then she looked up at the painting of George Washington and with grim determination instructed her servants, "Save that picture, if possible; if not possible, destroy it."[2] Dolley was not going to let the British play target practice on the founder of her country.

When the British arrived, they burned the White House to the ground, leaving behind only a skeleton of the Executive Mansion. But George Washington's portrait was saved,

The painting of George Washington was actually a copy and not the original.
So why was Dolley so determined to save a mere copy? It wasn't the painting,
but what it represented—American pride.

and years later, people would understand the importance of Dolley's forethought. The British could burn buildings, but they couldn't extinguish America's pride. Dolley Madison knew the power of symbols to convey hope and determination.

Dolley Payne Todd Madison was born on May 20, 1768, in Guilford County, North Carolina. She grew up as part of the decidedly unfashionable Religious Society of Friends, known as Quakers. As a Quaker, Dolley was required to dress in a plain black or gray dress with a white apron. A white bonnet covered her hair and a white handkerchief covered her bosom. It wasn't exactly flashy.

In 1790, Dolley married another Quaker named John Todd and had two children with him. Tragedy struck three years later, when a yellow fever epidemic hit Philadelphia and claimed Dolley's young son and her husband. Since women in the 1800s were not allowed to own property, Dolley had to fight her creditors just to keep the clothes on her back. She also lacked a steady income and therefore needed to remarry to support her surviving two-year-old son.

As a young, vivacious widow, the twenty-five-year-old Dolley did not remain single long. It seemed that whenever she walked outside, a trail of Philadelphia's most prominent bachelors would follow behind her. One such bachelor was prominent Congressman James Madison.[3] Usually shy, he was instantly smitten with Dolley and asked for her hand in marriage only months after they met.

Marriage to James meant that Dolley had to leave the Quaker religion, because, at the time, Quaker law forbade marriage to non-Quakers. Dolley didn't lose much sleep over that one: no more dark colors, covered bosoms, or boring bonnets. Free from the constraints of the strict Quaker religion, Dolley was finally free to have fun with fashion.

And oh, what fun she had! Dolley became easy to spot at a party. You just had to look for the green parrot she kept perched on her shoulder or the tall ostrich feathers bobbing up and down on top of the colorful silk turban she wrapped around her jet-black curls. Dolley always wore the latest French fashions: daringly low-cut, empire-waist dresses in silk and gauzy linen. She preferred festive colors like deep red (her favorite), or soft hues of sky blue, pink, lavender, and sunny yellow. Instead of appearing dripping in diamonds (the symbol of European aristocracy), Dolly wore white and black pearls. We call pearls "classic" today, but it was Dolley who made them the symbol of good taste.

In 1808, James Madison ran for president, and with Dolley by his side he couldn't lose. She threw parties to entice voters, left her calling card all over the city, and wrote to politicians' wives to ask for recipes—a clever ploy to enlist them as her allies.[4] As a savvy politician, Dolley used fashion as her symbol of power. When she walked into a room, she filled up space. Her plumed headdresses gave her height while the long trains of her dresses swept behind her. By the time Madison had won, his opponent, Charles C. Pinckney, dryly quipped, "I was beaten by Mr. and Mrs. Madison. I might have had a better chance had I faced Mr. Madison alone."[5]

Once she was First Lady, Dolley hosted weekly parties that became the talk of the town. Guests from all over the country showed up to discuss the latest news and help themselves to punch, cookies, fruit, and Mrs. Madison's "hot" new dessert—ice cream. (Oyster ice cream was her favorite flavor.)[6] In fact, so many politicians and their wives crammed shoulder to shoulder in the First Lady's elegant drawing rooms that the parties were called "squeezes."[7]

These squeezes served one very important purpose—they kept the peace. You know that painting where everyone is signing the Declaration of Independence and the Founding Fathers are looking like best buddies? Well, that's a bit of a lie. There was quite a lot of bickering in Washington in the early 1800s. In fact, if you didn't agree with someone's political views than you usually settled it by seeing who could shoot the fastest on the dueling field.[8] But people didn't wave guns at Dolley's parties. She could calm tempers as easily as disarming a ticking time bomb. When men started arguing over a political issue, she would simply interrupt the discussion with a wave of her white glove, a sly smile, and a call for more punch and cookies.

Dolley was like one of her decadent ice cream sundaes. You couldn't help but find her sweetness delicious. In a conversation with Henry Clay, he once complimented his hostess by saying "Everybody loves Mrs. Madison." Always quick witted, Dolley retorted, "That's because Mrs. Madison loves every-body."[9] That summed up why people were so drawn to Dolley: she made everyone feel comfortable, from poor farmers to posh aristocrats. Some call it charisma, but, really, it was her kindness that made her so loved.

After his second presidential term, Dolley and James retired to Montpelier, Virginia. She was so honored by the American people that she was given a token seat on the Congress floor and given franking privileges so that she could send letters without paying postage—a perk usually only given to former presidents.

When Dolley passed away in 1849, her funeral was one of the largest Washington had ever seen.[10] One senator referred to her as the "Queen of Hearts," a fitting title for a woman who gave her heart to a nation.[11]

## DOLLEY'S CHARM SCHOOL

1. **Never compare yourself to anyone else.** It will make you miserable. Dolley was not the prettiest woman at the party, but she was the one happiest in her own skin. One time when a politician's wife showed up wearing the same dress (a fashion catastrophe for the insecure) she complimented the woman by saying, "how much we think alike."[12]

2. **Remember people's names.** Dolley made it a habit of remembering everyone's name and his or her dislikes and likes. By remembering little things about people, she could more easily make conversation with guests.

3. **A conversation starter is the perfect accessory.** Dolley walked into every party with her parrot on her shoulder and a book in her hand (usually a book by an American author). She used the book as an icebreaker to make conversation with shyer guests.

4. **If people start to bicker, serve punch.** Or ice cream. Or whatever dessert will sweeten the atmosphere.

# Dolley Madison Style

Empire-waist dress

Parrot

Jet-black
curly hair

Smiles

Feathered
fascinator

Oyster
ice cream

Colors

Turban

Black
pearls

# Comfort
# Meets
# Elegance

# COCO CHANEL
## 1883–1971

*The most courageous act is still to think for yourself. Aloud.*

COCO CHANEL

If you have ever hated how runway models sometimes look like overdressed cyborgs, then you might be channeling your inner Chanel. Chanel always preferred simplicity to showiness. She hated anything that drew too much attention to the clothes, and not enough to the woman wearing them. Her life was dramatic enough without clothing complicating it.

As a young girl, Gabrielle Bonheur Chanel had a bit of a dark side. One of her favorite pastimes was to romp in hushed graveyards. She once said, "The first people to whom I opened my heart were the dead."[1] Death was something Chanel had to be comfortable with early on in life. When she was just eleven years old, her mother died, after which her dad left her like a bag of rotten potatoes on the doorsteps of an abbey in Abazine, France.

As an orphan in the abbey, Chanel's life became a monotonous routine of grasping hands together in prayer and dressing always in the same itchy black uniform with a starched white collar. Chanel would later recall, "I was in mourning all the time."[2] Fortunately, the nuns taught her to sew and that worked out pretty well for her.

Her first job was as a seamstress mending army officer uniforms. At night, she sang at a local music hall. From one of her most popular songs—"Qui qu'a vu Coco," a fast-tempo ditty about a girl who lost her dog—she got the nickname "Coco." It was a fitting name for such a spunky young woman. Chanel was always on the move. She rode horses bareback

at breakneck speeds, caught a twelve-pound fish, cut her hair short, tanned her skin (unheard of then), and always wore clothes that made her feel free.[3]

Most women in the early part of the twentieth century wore undergarments that curved their body into a shape it was never intended to make. They wore blouses with puffy sleeves and endless pleats, lace, and pin tucks paired with long, tight skirts over tight-fitting corsets. Most women looked like mermaids thrown onto land; they could barely walk, not to mention breathe. Chanel was having none of that. Instead, she skipped the corset and wore loose shirts, ties, and jackets stolen from boyfriends' closets. At least in men's clothes she could move.

Chanel took a lot of fashion inspiration from the men in her life. The love of her life, Boy Capel, wore loose-fitting sweaters that Chanel admired for their comfort. One day, she stole a sweater from Boy's closet to stay warm, but to add a bit more *je ne sais quoi* to it, she took a pair of scissors, cut the sweater up the middle, added some ribbon and a collar, and created an instant chic dress.[4] Other women wanted one just like it so Chanel opened her own shop in Paris where she outfitted the most stylish ladies.

During World War I, she knew that fashion had to be even more down to earth. As the men were away at war, more and more women found themselves working in hospitals, factories, farms, and driving cars. Women needed a comfortable material that did not confine the body. Enter jersey—the cheap, no frills, Cinderella of fabric. At the time, jersey was only used in underwear. No respectable society woman would abandon her silk, wool, or cashmere for the material used to cover (gasp!) bottoms. But times were changing and Chanel sensed it better than anyone. She created a series of simple dresses using lightweight jersey fabric, paired them with two-toned heels, long pearls, and *voilà . . .* instant chic.

Then she staged a fashion *coup d'état*: she chose black crepe de chine, a fabric that at this time was only worn by aged dowagers in mourning, and, armed with the scissors that she always wore on

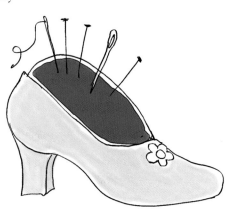

a long white ribbon around her neck, she nipped, tucked, pinned, and whipped out a simple black sheath in ninety minutes flat.[5] *Vogue* called the little black dress "Chanel's Ford" and it soon became every gal's go-to for looking effortlessly pulled together.

Yet Chanel's biggest success came because she had a nose for it—literally. In 1918, an old Renaissance manuscript was discovered during renovations of a chateau's library. This manuscript contained the secret perfume formula worn by Queen Marie de Medici. Chanel paid six thousand francs ($10,000 by today's

"To be elegant is to wear clothes that permit you to move, elegantly, gracefully, comfortably."[6] —Coco Chanel

standard) for the manuscript and hired perfumery Ernest Beaux to improve upon it. This perfume was named Chanel No. 5 after Chanel's favorite number.

Then she sprayed the perfume everywhere. Have you ever run into those department store ladies that attack you with the perfume samples? Well, Chanel invented that game. You couldn't go out to dinner with her without her spraying her perfume on everyone. People kept asking, "What is that delicious smell?" Followed by, "And where can I buy it?" Today, Chanel No. 5 is bought every fifty-five seconds, making it the world's best-selling perfume.[7]

Chanel continued to work until the day she died: nipping, poking, pinning, and trimming fabric into comfortable and elegant fashions. Her styles changed, but her intent stayed the same. To Chanel, fashion was always freedom. She designed clothes for real women in real life. Clothes that allowed a woman to ride a bike, run after a train, and dance a mean tango. So if one day you reach into your closet for that little black dress, jersey cardigan, or long pearls, and feel like the coolest creature alive, then repeat after me: "Thank you, Chanel."

# Coco Chanel Style

Quilted bag

Chanel No. 5

Bobbed hair

Groomed eyebrows

Pearls

Camellia

Neutral colors

Boater hat

Two-toned pumps

Little black dress

Bouclé jacket

Costume jewelry

# THE STORY OF THE LITTLE BLACK DRESS (LBD)

In the **1930s,** flappers like Josephine Baker wore black beaded dresses.

In **1884,** Madame Avegno caused a scandal in Paris when she allowed John Singer Sargent to paint her in a low-cut black dress. At the time, black was only worn while in mourning.

In **1926,** Chanel designed a simple black sheath dress dubbed "Chanel's Ford" because, like the Model T cars of the time, it was comfortable, versatile, and every woman could own one.

During the **1940s,** a boxier, more somber, version of the LBD was popular. This simpler version was due to wartime rationing that did not allow for expensive embellishments on clothing.

In the **1950s,** designer Christian Dior created a new version of the LBD with a full skirt and cinched waist.

In the later part of the **1960s and early 1970s,** LBD hemlines went shorter—way shorter. The LBD minidress was born.

In the **1990s,** the LBD took on a streamlined look with a more body-hugging design. It was sometimes paired with combat boots and fishnets for an edgier, grunge style.

**Today,** the LBD is still the classic go-to.

In **1961,** Audrey Hepburn made the slimmed-down version of the LBD the epitome of Hollywood glamour.

# East Styles West

HOLLYWOOD

# ANNA MAY WONG
## 1905–1961

*I want to become mentally and spiritually all that is possible for me to be.*
ANNA MAY WONG

"Cut!" yelled director Lee Ephraim. His leading lady, Anna May Wong, was walking all wrong. Anna May was playing the role of a Chinese girl named Min Lee and Ephraim wanted her to walk with the "short, hesitant steps"[1] of a geisha girl (female hostesses who entertained men with songs, instruments, dances, and conversation). A geisha girl was required to be gentle, charming, and always demure. Only one problem: geishas were Japanese, not Chinese. Anna May had to delicately explain to Ephraim that Chinese girls took normal steps when they walked.[2] It wouldn't be the last time she would have to educate directors about her Chinese culture.

Anna May Wong was born on January 3, 1905, on the outskirts of Los Angeles' Chinatown. As a young girl, Anna May spent long days in her father's laundry business, lifting an eight-pound iron to press clothes and trying not to fall on the wet, slippery floor. Once the clothes were washed and pressed, Anna May dragged them up the hill in a wicker basket under the Los Angeles sun. Sometimes, customers would feel bad for the wide-eyed child with the long braids down her back and give her a penny or two. Once Anna May had collected five pennies in her sweaty palm, she had enough to go to the movies.[3]

The movies Anna May saw were not like the movies today. They were black and white and only ten to twelve minutes long. These first movies were called silent films.

Before the invention of artificial lighting, directors needed natural sunlight to shoot. Consequently, Los Angeles became the center of the movie industry because it had more days of sunlight than other parts of the country.

The term "silent" is a bit misleading because although people did not speak in the films, the theaters still boomed with the sound of pianos, violins, and organs. A major silent film would even be accompanied by a full orchestra playing an original film score. Instead of using dialogue, the actors used dramatic facial gestures to communicate emotions. Anna May would run home and practice capturing those wild emotions in front of her mirror.[4]

Often skipping school to hang around the movie sets in her neighborhood, Anna May eventually became such a regular fixture at one set that the actors started calling her the "curious Chinese child."[5] All her persistence eventually paid off when she was cast as one of three hundred extras in the silent film, *The Red Lantern*. Anna May was so excited for her first (admittedly small) role that she ran home and covered her face with her mother's rice powder. When the makeup man saw Anna May, he laughed and sat Anna May down to remove her ghostly makeup.[6]

Anna May continued to land small roles until she got her first starring role at age nineteen in *Toll of the Sea* (1922). In it, she played a Chinese girl named Lotus Flower who falls in love with an American man washed up on the shore. In real life, California law forbade interracial marriages and most people did not accept couples of mixed race. Not only could the leading man never marry Anna May, he could not even kiss her on screen as Hollywood's production codes forbade any on-screen kissing between two people of different races.[7] This meant that whenever there was a love story Anna May usually lost the lead role to non-Chinese actresses, even when the role called for a Chinese woman. Hollywood studios would use makeup foundation called "yellow face" to make their white stars look

Anna May often took everyday objects and turned them into her own fashion statements. She put cornflowers behind each ear and even turned an embroidered piano cover into a dress.

Asian. They even applied gum arabic to the corners of the eye and used tape to pull the eyelids back.

Because Anna May often could not play the same characters as white actresses, she was cast as either one of two extremes: the deceitful and cruel "dragon lady" or a submissive and often helpless "china doll."

Eventually Anna May got tired of these stereotypical roles and started to turn down parts that cast Asians in an unrealistic light.

Hoping for less discrimination, in 1928, she left the US and acted in movies throughout Europe. There she was admired for more than just her acting abilities: Europeans also appreciated her fabulous sense of style. In Paris, women copied Anna May by wearing Chinese gowns, silk turbans, and long capes. In London, girls cut their hair like Anna May—blunt, short bangs, with hair pulled back in a bun—and tinted their faces a pale ochre color to get the "Wong complexion."[8]

Anna May eventually returned to the US, more confident and proud of her Chinese heritage. When studio executives asked her to cut her hair for one of her roles, she refused. She did not want to Americanize her look.[9] She also insisted on wearing traditional Chinese clothing. She caused a sensation when she showed up for one party wearing a stunning cheongsam, (pronounced chung sum).[10] A cheongsam is a long dress usually embroidered with symbols and flowers.

For her publicity shot for the movie, *Limehouse Blues*, Anna May wore a black dress adorned with a gold and silver sequin dragon.

ANNA MAY WONG

49

*(See "Anna May Style" on page 51)* For one publicity shot, Anna May wore a cheongsam-style gown embroidered with dragons—the symbol of power in China.

By 1934, she had secured her place as a fashion icon when the Mayfair Mannequin Society of New York voted her the "world's best dressed woman."[11]

A famous poem by Rudyard Kipling described attitudes toward eastern cultures: "Oh, East is East and West is West, and never the twain shall meet."[12] (A twain is old English for "two.") Anna May disagreed with these lines because she felt she had to straddle both worlds—her heritage (the East) and her Hollywood career (the West). She explained that she was "born and raised in the eastern world, but the western world is present in every moment of my life."[13] Anna May knew that she couldn't change the world overnight but, through fashion, she could combine exotic orientalism with Hollywood glamour. Through fashion, she bridged the gap between East and West.

## ANNA MAY'S STYLE TIPS

Anna May toured the United States lecturing on eastern beauty secrets. Some of her tips were a bit silly. (She recommended staring at goldfish to strengthen the eyes and sleeping on a leather pillow to prevent wrinkles.) But many of her style tips would still hold true today.

1. Comb your hair instead of brushing it. This is especially true if hair is wet because combing it causes less breakage.

2. Don't wash your hair every day. Washing your hair every day strips out the natural oils and can leave hair dry and brittle.

3. Massage vegetable oil into scalp and hair. Vegetable oil can be used as a conditioner. (Coconut oil is the best.) Leave in for an hour and then rinse.

4. Wear blunt bangs. (You don't have to cut your hair to replicate a blunt bang. Use clip-on hair extensions to add bangs to any hairstyle.)

5. Adorn the hair with flowers and jewels. They can add just the right amount of playfulness to any hairstyle.

# Anna May Style

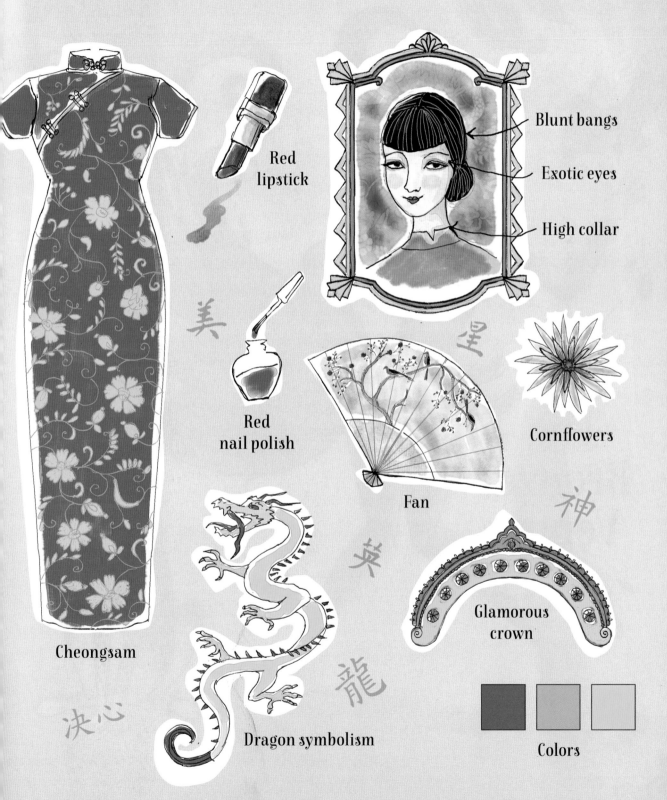

Red
lipstick

Blunt bangs

Exotic eyes

High collar

美

星

神

英

龍

決心

Red
nail polish

Fan

Cornflowers

Cheongsam

Dragon symbolism

Glamorous
crown

Colors

# The Bronze Venus

# JOSEPHINE BAKER
## 1906–1975

*Beautiful? It's all a question of luck. I was born with good legs.*
*As for the rest . . . beautiful, no. Amusing, yes.*

JOSEPHINE BAKER

It was 1926 and her opening night at Folies Bergère, the most popular dance hall in Paris. Costume designers had presented Josephine Baker with sketch after sketch of the most sumptuous gowns dripping with feathers and jewels. Josephine turned them all down. She wanted something fun. Something different. Feathers wouldn't cut it.

The curtain was raised to reveal a painted backdrop of a jungle with hanging vines over clear, blue water. The drums thumped out a slow, steady beat as Josephine crept behind a fallen tree prop like a graceful tiger about to pounce on its prey. Suddenly, she sprang forward, barefoot and gyrating her hips in whip-cracking speed. Around her waist . . . a girdle hanging with bananas.

The audience stood up and roared with laughter. When she was later asked why she dressed so silly, Josephine said it was because she wanted people to "shake off their worries the way a dog shakes off his fleas."[1] It certainly worked. Women cut their hair short, danced the Charleston, and felt as free as Josephine. Advertisers took notice too. They used Josephine's face to sell skin lotion, dolls, recipes, and summer vacations. White women tanned their skin to get "Bakerskin" or bought "Bakerfix" to copy Josephine's face-framing spit curls. For the first time in France, being black was beautiful.

Born in 1906 as Freda Josephine McDonald, Josephine had come a long way from her childhood home in St. Louis's segregated ghetto. Her family was so poor that during the winter months she scavenged for food in garbage cans[2] and fashioned shoes made from rolled newspapers[3] or scratchy coal sacks.[4] In May 1917, race riots erupted near her neighborhood. Mobs of whites stormed the streets of East St. Louis, destroying property and killing thirty-nine blacks. Josephine fled the city with her mother and siblings, later describing the scene as an "apocalypse" of "breathless figures that dashed in all directions."[5]

To forget the racial tensions, Josephine gave make-believe concerts in her basement singing atop orange crates.[6] Watching her, no one would have thought such a lanky weed of a girl would blossom into the mighty "Bronze Venus" and jazz babe sensation. Teased for her pointy knees and mocha colored skin, she was told that she danced "like a monkey" when she first performed the Charleston for New York theatergoers.[7] Josephine shook it off. The racial slurs couldn't keep a rare bird caged.

In 1925, she headed to Paris where she created an uproar at the Théâtre des Champs-Elysées. Wearing pink feathered skirts and ropes of pearls, Josephine kicked her legs up and swung her knees in and out to the hot new dance, "le Charleston." She went on to join the music hall Folies Bergère where she traded her feathers for her infamous banana skirt.

In Paris, Josephine fell in love with the clean, geometric lines of the popular art deco fashions. But she was not about to sit back and let designers dress her, as leading designer Paul Poiret learned the hard way. After inviting her to his private fashion show, he showed her dress after dress but Miss Baker seemed unimpressed. Finally, she asked for pen and paper. With a few staccato scratches of her pen, she sketched out a simple shift dress with a layer of fringe at the bottom. Everyone in the room was shocked by Josephine's audacity. Poiret was not. He turned to Josephine and said, "Thank you, Josephine. You are hired . . . I will call this dress 'La Robe Josephine Baker.'"[8] The dress, in shades of pale pink with two rows of fringe, became *the* dress among Paris's fashionable elite.

Josephine was the first female African American to star in an international motion picture, and she would go on to star in a total of seven films. In 1931, she recorded her hit song, "J'ai deux amours" (I have two loves). Josephine did have two loves: her childhood home in the United States of America and her new home in Paris. Unfortunately, the US was sometimes an unrequited love.

During one US tour, hotels refused to receive her. Accustomed to a red carpet treatment in Europe, Josephine declined to perform in any city that would not allow her to stay in

Military Style: Josephine wasn't afraid to bend gender roles. To resemble French men, she parted her short hair to one side and then added a top hat. When she appeared at the 1963 civil rights march on Washington, she wore her French Resistance uniform. Get her look with a military-style jacket or accessorize a shirt with military-style buttons.

their best hotels. She also demanded that theaters not segregate their audiences, and cities that did not comply with her wishes simply lost the chance to see her perform. Josephine knew her worth and demanded that audiences enjoy her performance together . . . regardless of skin color.

Like Cleopatra on her barge, Josephine cultivated her queenly image by dining on delicacies of cockscombs (the red crown of the rooster) and champagne,[9] accompanied by her perfumed pet pig.[10] She bought a fifty-room, fifteenth-century château, perched high on a rocky hill in France's Aquitaine region, and slept on a bed she claimed had once belonged to Marie Antoinette.[11] When not performing, she could be found flying airplanes,[12] strolling along the Champs-Elysées with her two pet leopards,[13] going to the opera with her pet cheetah,[14] or motoring around Paris in her copper-colored automobile (a rarity then).[15]

During World War II, she worked as a spy for the French Resistance—the people who fought the occupying Nazi forces. Decked out in feathers, she charmed Nazi soldiers into revealing enemy secrets and smuggled coded messages in invisible ink back to French Resistance leaders. Sometimes she pinned top-secret notes to her underwear, boldly assuming that authorities wouldn't dare strip-search "La Baker." (They never did.)[16]

As big as she lived, she loved even bigger. In the winter of 1938, during an economic depression in Paris, she rented a truck and traveled through the suburbs flinging potatoes, bread, coal, and toys to the poverty-stricken inhabitants.[17] Back in the US after the war, she gave speeches alongside Martin Luther King Jr., to promote racial equality, and gave benefit concerts to help

La Baker

desegregate the St. Louis school system. In the 1950s, Josephine began to adopt children of different ethnicities, twelve in total, whom she called "her rainbow tribe."[18]

In an age when African American women were not allowed to go to the same hair salons as white women, Josephine shimmied and shook her way into the hearts of millions. She racked up some two thousand marriage proposals, including a raja who offered to give up his harem for her.[19] Picasso mused that she had "coffee skin" and "a smile to end all smiles."[20] Hemingway remembered her as "the most sensational woman anyone ever saw."[21] He just might have been right.

# THE SECRET TO JOSEPHINE BAKER'S PIN CURLS

**Supplies**

• Hair clips

• Rattail comb

• Water

### Step 1
Before bedtime, wash and blow dry your hair on a cool setting until hair is only slightly damp.

### Step 4
Repeat with one-inch sections in rows across the crown of the head. Remember to twist hair in the same direction in each row.

### Step 5
Wrap your head in a scarf and sleep on pin curls. In the morning, take out the pins.

### Step 2
Using comb end, section out a one-inch chunk of hair and spritz with water. If you want to be really authentic, use spit instead of water.

### Step 3
Wind the hair around your finger, keeping it close to your head. Slide the curl off your finger and onto your head; secure with a hair clip or bobby pin.

# Josephine Baker Style

Pearls . . . lots of pearls

Feathers

Bananas

Drop-waist dress

T-strap shoes

Leopard clutch

Pin curls

Colors

Art deco earrings

Red lipstick

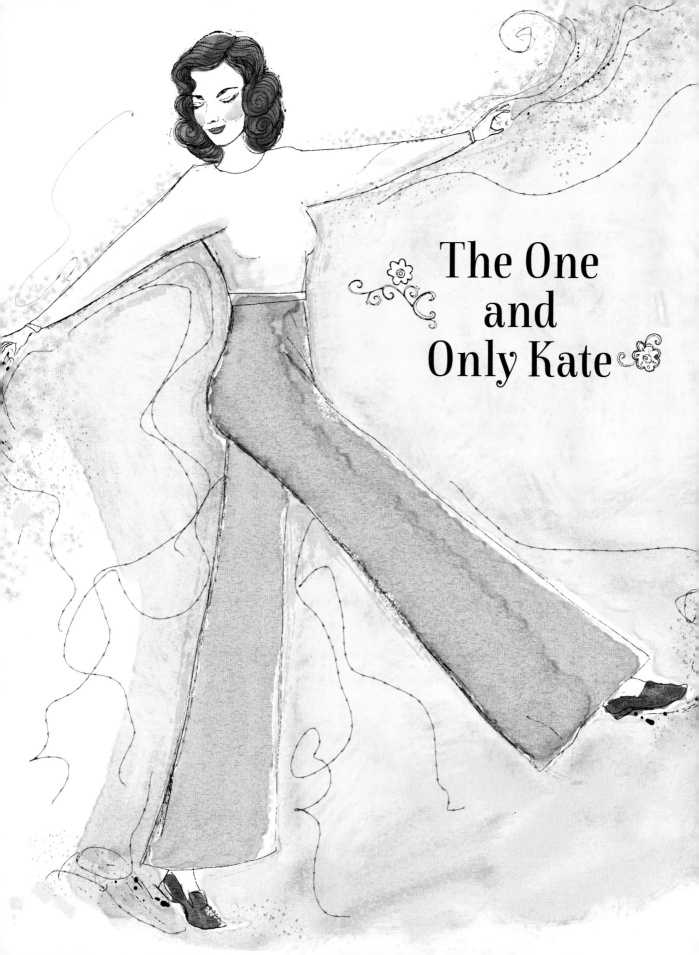

# The One
# and
# Only Kate

# KATHARINE HEPBURN
## 1907–2003

*If you obey all of the rules,*
*you miss all of the fun.*
KATHARINE HEPBURN

Something had to be done about Ms. Hepburn. The movie studio executives needed their leading lady to look like a lady. In the ultra-feminine 1930s and 40s, that meant pouty, bee-stung lips, bullet bras, girdles, garters, stockings, and, of course, a sensible skirt. Instead, the lanky Katharine Hepburn kept wearing those-crude looking pants called "jeans." It simply wouldn't do. Respectable ladies didn't wear jeans.

The studio executives took action. When Katharine was out of her dressing room, they stole her jeans. After she discovered the theft, Katharine threatened to walk out of her dressing room naked if she didn't get her jeans back. The executives held their ground. She wouldn't dare. Oh, but she would. Katharine stuck her aristocratic nose in the air and marched right out of her dressing room wearing nothing but silk underwear. The executives relented quicker than you can say "cut." They never tried that stunt again.[1]

Katharine Houghton Hepburn (known as Kathy to her family) had been crafting her tomboy-chic style since she was a freckle-faced, red-haired wisp of a girl. She wasn't about to mend her rebel ways now. At a time when most young ladies were only athletic enough to lift a teacup, Kathy was swan diving off cliffs and swinging golf clubs better than most prep-school boys. Her favorite rabble-rousing outfit was trousers and an oversized white shirt stolen from her brother Tom's closet. When she was eight, she lopped off all her hair and told her family to start calling her "Jimmy."[2]

It didn't take long for "Jimmy" to scandalize Hartford, Connecticut. Still, Kathy's parents didn't discourage their daughter's creative expression. When Katharine was sent home from school for wearing her brother's clothes, her mother promptly sent her back wearing the same outfit. Once a concerned neighbor called up Mrs. Hepburn to tell her that Kathy was climbing trees again. Her mother simply responded, "Yes, I know. Don't scare her. She doesn't know that it's dangerous."[3]

If Katharine Hepburn were going to confront danger, it certainly wouldn't be in high heels and stockings (which she called "the invention of the devil").[4] She wore little makeup and often swept her hair into a simple librarian bun or tucked it under a handkerchief. She always preferred practicality to panache. In an interview with Calvin Klein she confessed, "I realized long ago that skirts are hopeless. Anytime I hear a man say he prefers a woman in a skirt, I say, 'Try one. Try a skirt.'"[5]

Katharine would always favor pants over skirts. She showed up for rehearsals wearing baggy sweaters held together with safety pins and wide-legged trousers. One director even ordered her off stage until she put on a dress. She quickly found a

Katharine designed many of the dresses for her movie roles. She preferred luxurious fabrics that skimmed the body to tight-fitting clothes. She once said, "No matter how free women get, they always seem to be absolutely tied into asinine clothes."[6]

burlap bag backstage and fashioned it into a makeshift dress.[8] Everyone laughed (except the director).

Despite her casual style, her outfits always retained a feminine softness. If she wore a jacket, it would be cinched at the waist with pretty buttons. She wrote detailed notes to her costume designers and sketched out ideas on yellow, lined legal paper. Designer Edith Head knew best how to deal with the strong-willed Kate. She said, "One does not design for Miss Hepburn. One designs with her."[9]

Unfortunately, her brashness did not always win people over. After a series of movie flops in the 1930s, Katharine was labeled "box-office poison."[10] But whenever someone told Katharine she wasn't good enough, she ignored the criticism and only worked harder. She once said, "I think you should pretend you don't care."[11] Of course, she did care, but she never let others know it. Instead, she staged an epic comeback. Katharine went on to have a box-office hit in the *Philadelphia Story* (1940), and win four Best Actress Oscars.

Today, her carefree, windblown style looks ripped straight from a J.Crew catalog, but Katharine didn't have it so easy. In the 1940s, audiences preferred stars with soft curves and a dash of pin-up perkiness. Katharine was no cutie pie. She was brash. She was bold. She was always one hundred percent Katharine Hepburn.

## THE ONE-AND-ONLY-KATE STYLE TIPS

1. **Be comfortable.** Comfort is always in style, and Kate always dressed as if she were ready for a grand adventure. That meant pants that let her freely move her legs and a sensible pair of shoes for going the distance.

2. **Find a good tailor.** When Kate wore a dress she looked as comfortable as Aphrodite wearing sea foam. What was her secret? A good tailor. She hired a man's tailor to fit her trousers to her sleek frame and had her shoes custom made. She had at least thirty trousers in her closet, all patched, tailored, and mended.

3. **Stay fit.** Kate never sat still. She swam every morning outside, even in frigid temperatures, and followed it up with a tennis lesson and nine holes of golf. She did her own movie stunts and went boar hunting while filming in Africa. She even kept her hands busy during takes by knitting. At age forty, she took up jogging with Greta Garbo. At eighty-four, she could still do a headstand.

4. **Be real.** Kate could spot a phony like a shark smells blood in the water. When not on set, she didn't wear a stitch of makeup and kept her hair in a no-fuss bun. She rarely posed for pictures and gave interviews only reluctantly. If social networking had been around, you wouldn't have caught her oversharing. She was far too busy living life to make regular updates on it.

5. **Eat well, drink well.** Kate was obsessed with hydration and made sure all her friends went to the bathroom frequently. She ate five servings of vegetables a day with the occasional chocolate indulgence.

# Katharine Hepburn Style

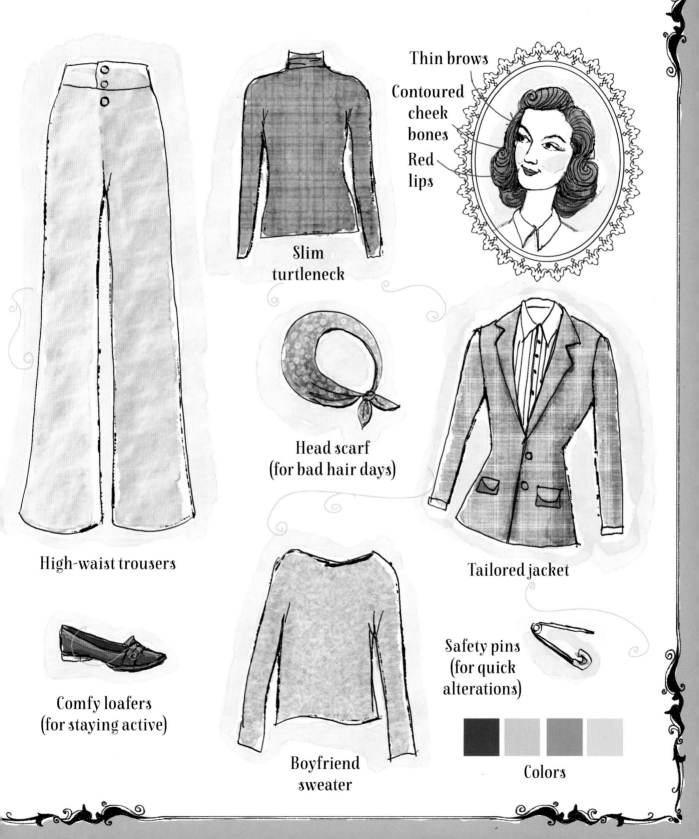

Thin brows

Contoured cheek bones

Red lips

Slim turtleneck

Head scarf
(for bad hair days)

High-waist trousers

Tailored jacket

Comfy loafers
(for staying active)

Safety pins
(for quick alterations)

Boyfriend sweater

Colors

# WHO WORE THE PANTS?

Throughout history, women wearing pants has caused some ruckus. The following ladies abandoned customs (and their skirts) for the right to wear pants.

In **450 BCE,** Queen Medea, a princess from the Caucasus region wore pants. Both ancient Persian men and women then adopted the fashion.

In **1431,** Joan of Arc was charged with heresy and wearing pants. (At the time, wearing pants in France was illegal if you were a woman.) The heresy charges became difficult to prove but her cross-dressing did not. She was burnt at the stake.

In **1771,** Marie Antoinette shocked the staid French court when she dared to wear breeches—the slim fitting riding pants worn only by men.

*If you are riding like a man, dressed like a man . . . I find it dangerous as well as bad for bearing children.*[1]
MARIA THERESA,
MARIE ANTOINETTE'S MOTHER

In **1851,** Elizabeth Smith Miller abandoned her heavy petticoats and skirts in favor of wide-legged pants called Turkish pantaloons. Elizabeth Stanton, an activist for women's rights, adored Miller's pants and wore them to visit her friend, Amelia Bloomer, who also admired the pants. Bloomer began to wear them as well and advocated wearing pants in her newspaper *The Lily*— the first newspaper edited by a woman. The pant-wearing trend caught on and pants became known as "Bloomers." Women who wore them were ridiculed as immoral.

From **1859 to the 1890s,** while Amelia Bloomer grew tired of the ridicule and stopped wearing bloomers, other women did not. Bloomers made it easier for women to ride bicycles and became popular sports attire.

From **1890 to 1940** the "Bloomer Girls" took over baseball. These mostly female teams (some teams had a male pitcher) challenged men's teams throughout the country while wearing the loose-fitting bloomers named after suffragette leader Amelia Bloomer.

*"The costume of women should be suited to her wants and necessities."*[2]
AMELIA BLOOMER, 1848

In the **1930s,** German actress Marlene Dietrich caused a scandal when she wore a pantsuit. Katharine Hepburn also later shocked studio executives by wearing jeans.

In **1934,** the first women's jeans were manufactured by Levi Strauss & Co. and sold to women working on ranches.

**1908 to 1911:** French designer Paul Poiret, inspired by Asian designs, created fashionable pants that made the cover of *Vogue* in 1913. Women love them.

From **1939 to 1945,** with husbands off fighting in World War II, female factory workers wore pants and utility suits for safety.

In the **1940s and 1950s,** fashion designer Sonja de Lennart designed three-quarter-length pants called capris. Actress Grace Kelly became one of the first celebrities to wear them.

In the **1960s,** skinny pants or "drainpipe pants" became popular after Audrey Hepburn wore them in her 1957 hit movie *Funny Face*.

In the **1970s,** bell-bottoms became the staple of hippie chic after actress Cher wore them on her popular TV show *Sony and Cher*.

In the **1980s,** high-waisted jeans were made popular by supermodels like Cindy Crawford.

In **1993,** the ban that prohibited women from wearing pants on the US Senate floor was finally lifted.

**Today,** girls can wear capris, jeans, slacks, sweatpants . . . or any pants they choose. Thanks, ladies!

# FRIDA KAHLO
## 1907–1954

*Feet, what do I need them for if I have wings to fly.*

FRIDA KAHLO

On a hot, dry night in April 1953, Frida Kahlo lay confined to her four-poster bed, barely able to walk. A mirror hanging on the underside of the bed's canopy reflected a woman smiling through the pain. She wore a garden of flowers in her braided hair and a bright silk shirt with a square collar, chain-stitched with a sunny yellow pattern of interweaving squares and crisscrosses. Frida was wearing a Tehuana, the native dress of Tehuantepec women.[1] Frida identified with these strong, independent women.

That night, Frida was to have her first solo art exhibition in Mexico, but her doctors had forbade her from leaving her bed. Frida had always dreamed of seeing her paintings displayed in a show in her home country. She certainly was not going to miss it now. Yes, she would follow doctor's orders. She would stay in bed. But no one said her bed had to say put.

Frida arrived for her show by ambulance and was carried to the middle of the gallery where her bed had been installed. Over two hundred friends and admirers crowded around her, talking about art and singing bawdy Mexican ballads. Above her, a skeleton sculpture hung from the bed's canopy, seeming to dance every time Frida shook with laughter.[2] One friend commented it was "the kind of performance that she loved—colorful, surprising, intensely human, and a little morbid."[3]

Frida Kahlo de Rivera was born on July 6, 1907, outside of Mexico City in the small village of Coyoacán. Her father was a photographer who had immigrated to Mexico from Germany and her mother was of mixed American Indian and Spanish ancestry.

From the time Frida was born she was surrounded with colors. She lived in a cobalt blue house (La Casa Azul) nestled in a jungle of leafy green fauna and a vivid kaleidoscope of dahlias in red, fushia, orange, yellow, pink, and white.

Unfortunately, much of Frida's childhood was also colored by sickness. When she was six years old she contracted polio, an infectious disease that often caused paralysis. She survived, but was left with one leg shorter than the other. Forced to walk with a limp, the kids in school teased her and called her "peg-leg Frida."[4] But she refused to be treated differently. She swam and climbed trees, even though only boys did such things in her village. To hide her malformed leg, she wore long skirts or sometimes a man's suit.

When Frida was just nineteen she suffered another misfortune when she was in a horrible bus accident. The injuries left her near death. Her spine and pelvis were broken in three places. Her right leg, collarbone, and ribs were broken, and her foot was dislocated and crushed. Her injuries were so severe that one friend commented that her doctors had to "put her back together in sections as if they were making a photomontage."[5] (A combination of photos assembled together.) During the many months confined to her bed, Frida borrowed the paints her father used to tint photographs. Because she could not move, her

"I paint flowers so they will not die."

mother installed a mirror above her bed so she could paint herself. Thus began Frida's love of painting self-portraits.[6] She would later say, "I paint myself because I am so often alone and because I am the subject I know best."[7]

Frida slowly recovered enough to leave La Casa Azul. Although the accident and her childhood polio would always cause her to walk with a limp, it did not stop her from going out dancing late into the night. At one party in 1928, Frida met a famous artist named Diego Rivera. It wasn't long before the two had fallen in love and were married. The next year, the couple moved to the United States so Diego could paint a mural in San Francisco.

In 1929, Frida arrived in the US with her husband, wearing one of her colorful Mexican dresses and her hair piled into a crown of braids, flowers, and wrinkled scarves. Most Americans didn't know what to make of Frida's style. The fashion at the time was bobbed hair, mid-calf–length skirts, tight sweaters in ultrafeminine pastels, and very few accessories. Then along came Frida Kahlo with her long braided hair, jewel-colored dresses, and enough rings, bracelets, and necklaces to fill a sultan's treasure chest. One observer described the jingling of her many metal bangles, rings, dangling earrings, and rope necklaces as "a cathedral gone mad."[8]

People would even follow her on the streets because she was dressed so vibrantly. Sometimes kids ran up to her and asked where the circus was.[9] Most shocking of all, her eyebrows were so bushy that they connected together like two wings of a bird. The style of the time was to pluck eyebrows into a thin line, but Frida even used a pencil to make her brows appear thicker.[10] Like an exotic bird in a sea of pigeons, Frida didn't care if she

Texture and color always had a deeper meaning to Frida in both what she wore and what she painted. She saw green as "soft, kind light," blue as " . . . electricity and purity. Love . . . ," yellow as "more madness and mystery." But her favorite was fuchsia, which she called "blood of a prickly pear, the most vivid and ancient."[11]

stood out. She was proud of her Mexican heritage and her Mexican clothing.

As her old injuries continued to plague her, she would channel her pain into her paintings. Frida's paintings were like weird dreams—full of things that didn't seem to belong together until you thought about their meaning as a whole. People at the time called it surrealism—painting as a way to channel the unconscious mind, but Frida never thought her art was surrealism. Frida said, "I never paint dreams or nightmares. I paint my own reality."[12]

In 1933, Frida and her husband moved back to Mexico where she became more and more famous for her paintings. People all over Europe also fell in love with her exotic fashions. In 1939, French *Vogue*, the most popular fashion magazine of the time, put Frida's hands with all her rings on the cover.[13] That same year, one of the most famous designers of the time, Elsa Schiaparelli, designed her own take on Frida's style that she titled, La Robe Madame Rivera.[14]

Sadly, as Frida's fame grew, her health deteriorated. The pains in her spine and foot from the bus accident increased to the point where she was forced to wear a steel corset. She had over thirty operations

In 1939, the Louvre in Paris bought Frida's self-portrait, *The Frame*. It was the first contemporary painting by a Mexican artist in their collection.

The bus accident prevented Frida from having children. Instead, she surrounded herself with pets: monkeys, parrots, and small dogs.

to fix her broken body and eventually her leg had to be amputated. Of course, even Frida's prosthetic boot had style. It was bright red and decorated with embroidery and bells. Frida did not complain about her disabilities. She said, "I am not sick. I am broken. But I am happy to be alive as long as I can paint."[15] Frida painted until she could no longer hold up her brush. On July 13, 1954, she died in La Casa Azul. Her last painting was a still life of cut watermelon. In the corner she wrote "Viva la Vida" (Long Live Life).

Toward the end of her life Frida kept a diary where she doodled dancing skeletons and wrote her innermost thoughts. On one page she drew a tree, filling it with thin, spiny branches reaching like hands to the sky. Underneath her drawing, she wrote the words from one of her favorite songs, "Tree of Hope stand firm."[16] Frida Kahlo at her core was like a solid oak tree. Her delicate branches could break, but the roots would always stay firmly planted in the ground. Her long dresses may have hid her physical weaknesses, but also allowed her to stand tall and be proud of her Mexican culture.

Today, Frida's fashion influence can be seen in "boho chic" embroidered dresses paired with braided hairstyles. But Frida's fashion sense was so much more than hippie chic defiance. In many ways, her festive clothing and flowered hair adornments were a celebration of life—a celebration of beauty, of art, and most importantly, courageous self-expression.

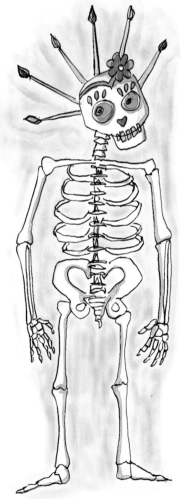

# MAKE A FRIDA-STYLE FLOWER CROWN

## Supplies

- Elastic band that matches your hair color
- Scissors
- Fabric glue
- Craft flowers

### Step 1

Measure stretched elastic around your head and cut it ½ inch longer than that length.

### Step 2

If the craft flowers have wires, cut the wires off and bend the extra so that it lays flush to the flower.

### Step 3

Glue the flower to the elastic band. Repeat with enough flowers to cover the crown.

### Step 4

Hand stitch or knot the ends of the band together.

### Tips

*You can also use a plain metal or plastic headband if you find elastics uncomfortable. Use craft flowers that are not so heavy they will fall off the elastic after they are glued on.*

# Frida Kahlo Style

Hoop earrings

Flowers

Braids

Lace shawl

Embroidered shirt

Long necklace

Lots and lots of rings

Long silk skirt

Embroidered sack bag

Jewel colors

# That Monroe Magic

# MARILYN MONROE
## 1926–1962

*I make it a point to stay the way*
*I want to be.*

MARILYN MONROE

A gust of wind lifting up your dress would usually be considered a serious wardrobe malfunction . . . unless, of course, you're Marilyn Monroe. On September 15, 1955, at 1:00 AM, Marilyn Monroe stood over a subway grate between Lexington Avenue and Fifty-Second Street waiting for such a gust of wind to do the unthinkable. She was filming for her movie *The Seven Year Itch*. The movie and her character are hardly remembered, but the dress . . . the dress is still the most recognizable dress in Hollywood today. It was an ivory colored halter-top dress that crisscrossed her waist and flowed into hand-sewn knife pleats. When the subway's hot air blew up, the delicate material billowed around Marilyn's body like molten liquid.

In the following weeks, replicas of Marilyn's dress flew out of department stores. A monster-sized billboard of a laughing Marilyn in her unforgettable dress flying skyward was placed high above Times Square. New Yorkers strained their necks upward to view the risqué billboard. Marilyn had only begun to shake up the fashion world.

Marilyn Monroe was born as Norma Jeane Mortenson on June 1, 1926, in Los Angeles. Her father abandoned the family before she was born and her mother suffered from depression and possibly schizophrenia, making it impossible for her to care for

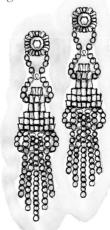

Marilyn. So Marilyn spent most of her childhood bouncing from foster home to foster home, or sometimes living in an orphanage.

As a young girl, she could see the water tower branded with the RKO Studios logo from her orphanage's bedroom window. RKO's logo at the time was a tall radio tower transmitting its signal like a beacon of hope. Marilyn would stare up at RKO's logo and dream about someday becoming a Hollywood star.[1]

In 1945, when she was nineteen, those dreams began to take shape. She posed for a wartime photo shoot while working in an airplane factory, and that picture of a freshly scrubbed, smiling girl holding up a screwdriver to an airplane propeller led to her first job as a clothing model. But Marilyn had much bigger dreams than modeling skirts for department store ads. In 1946 she got her first contract with Twentieth Century Fox. With Hollywood in her grasp, she changed her named to Marilyn Monroe and dyed her brown hair platinum blonde. While most of her first roles were one-liners or nonspeaking roles, Marilyn worked hard, studying acting and staying up late practicing lines.

Her hard work eventually paid off. She got her first big break in 1950 when she starred as the mistress of an aging criminal in *The Asphalt Jungle*. In 1953, she played a gold digger and showgirl named Lorelei Lee in *Gentlemen Prefer Blondes*. In one unforgettable scene, Marilyn sang "Diamonds Are a Girl's Best Friend" in a now iconic, hip-hugging, bubblegum pink dress and pink gloves. (See the dress on p. 86) Marilyn received rave reviews and that same year she was named the "Fastest Rising Star" by *Photoplay* magazine.[2]

Despite her success, many of Marilyn's first roles portrayed her as less than intelligent. In real life, she had a sharp mind and a wicked sense of humor. Although she had dropped out of high school, she was always intent on improving herself and took classes in literature and history at the University of California, Los Angeles.[3]

In her spare time, she listened to classical music, wrote poetry, and was an avid reader.[5] Although improving her craft was always a top priority, she also valued improving her mind. She said, "I once wanted to prove myself by being a great actress. Now I want to prove that I'm a person. Then maybe I'll be a great actress."[6]

Marilyn's independence came through in her style choices. When the stars of the film *How to Marry a Millionaire* were asked to wear the latest trend of full skirts and cinched waists, they all agreed. All except Marilyn.[7] Marilyn knew her body. Anything that made her look like a head popping out of a circus tent might work for a skinny girl, but it did nothing for her. Instead, she insisted on curve hugging dresses that fit within an inch of her life. (She had to be sewn into most of her dresses.)[8] To keep in shape, she took ice baths to get her blood flowing[9] and lifted weights (unheard of then).[10]

Marilyn was always comfortable with her hourglass figure and once told reporters, "I don't want to be bone thin, and I make it a point to stay the way I want to be."[11]

Marilyn's fashion sense may have been fun and girly, but she was also a complex and deeply private person. When asked during an interview if the tailored, black suit she was wearing was the "new Marilyn" she quipped, "No, I am the same person, but it's a different suit."[12] Marilyn never took fashion (or herself) too seriously and the world loved her for it.

Clothing allowed Marilyn to feel protected but could not hide her pain. On the outside she appeared confident and in control, batting her false eyelashes and blowing air kisses to the camera. On the inside . . . Marilyn had some serious demons. In letters to friends she repeatedly wrote, "I wish that I was dead."[13] Marilyn was battling depression.[14]

Despite the numerous white replicas, Marilyn's iconic dress was actually ivory. At the time, stars rarely wore white on film because it looked gray under the powerful studio lights. The dress was purchased by actress Debbie Reynolds in 1971 and sold at auction for 4.6 million dollars in 2011. Over the years, it has darkened and is now a light beige color.

Marilyn's final years were as bumpy as a derailed train. She attempted suicide several times but friends always came to her rescue.[15] Then on August 5, 1962, she was found lying on her bed, dead from a drug overdose.

Despite her tragic ending, Marilyn has become the epitome of classic Hollywood style. At a time when most women wore button down Peter Pan collars and staid dresses that hid their bodies, Marilyn put a little va-va-voom into the fashion world. Her white dress is the most recognizable dress in fashion history and her platinum blonde hair has become the iconic symbol for glamour. Movie stars and musicians have copied her look, from Madonna to Lindsay Lohan. Still, no one today can rock a white dress quite like Marilyn could. Her fashion choices were always fun because at heart, Marilyn was just a kid—a kid with a dream and one glamorous sense of style.

## Work Every Curve

# FOREVER MARILYN STYLE TIPS

1. **Love your curves.** Marilyn never wore baggy shirts or shapeless dresses. If you have an hourglass figure, try dresses cinched in at the waist that accentuate curves instead of hiding them.

2. **Get Hollywood glam hair.** Just as she styled her curvaceous body, Marilyn created a classic feminine style with her hair. To get Marilyn Monroe curls, wrap the hair under and around the finger forming a barrel. (A) Pin the curl to the root of the head with a hair clip or bobby pin. (B) Hairspray the hair and then wrap in a scarf for thirty minutes. Remove pins . . . and voilà, instant Hollywood glamour.

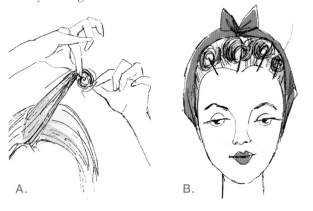

A.                B.

3. **Diamonds really are a girl's best friend.** Okay, maybe not diamonds, but a little bling never hurt anyone. Try a rhinestone bracelet or chandelier earrings to add that extra bit of sparkle. Just don't overdo it. Marilyn believed, "Flashy earrings, necklaces, and bracelets detract from a ladies' looks."[16]

4. **Just roll out of bed.** Marilyn never tried too hard to impress the fashion police. She mastered the "undone" look, often showing up for press conferences with tousled hair and no makeup.[17]

5. **Have a Marilyn moment.** Marilyn was the most lovable when she was making people laugh. If she screwed up, she made it look like it was on purpose. Embarrassing moments don't need to be embarrassing. So if you ever find a gust of wind exposing what you didn't mean to expose . . . laugh it off and the world will laugh with you.

# Marilyn Monroe Style

Cashmere cardigan
(flower at neck)

Diamonds

Silk clutch

Pencil skirt

White fur stole

Peep-toe shoes

Platinum hair

Mole

Curve-hugging dress

Air kisses

Bullet bra

Colors

That Is
So Audrey

# AUDREY HEPBURN
## 1929–1993

*I believe that happy girls are the prettiest girls.*

AUDREY HEPBURN

It was not love at first sight. It was the summer of 1953 and Audrey Hepburn couldn't wait to meet Paris's hottest fashion designer, Hubert de Givenchy.[1] In a white T-shirt and ballet slippers, she bounced up the winding, marble staircase of Givenchy's eighteenth-century mansion, gracefully taking two steps at a time. But when Givenchy laid eyes on Hepburn, his towering six-foot-seven-inch frame slumped forward in disappointment. He had been expecting the *other* Hepburn—actress Katharine Hepburn. Instead, this short-haired, long-limbed, coltish creature with the biggest feet he had ever seen (size ten!) stood before him. Worst of all, he had never heard of her. In 1953, Audrey's first big movie, *Roman Holiday*, had yet to be released.

Givenchy politely hid his regret and declined to design the clothing for her upcoming movie, *Sabrina*. He was far too busy preparing his winter collection to design dresses for an unknown actress. While most actresses would have thrown a diva-sized hissy fit, Audrey simply asked him if she could take something ready-made from one of his previous shows. Givenchy agreed. She was, after all, very charming.

Audrey dove into the clothing racks like Cinderella trading her rags for a princess ball gown. She chose a black cocktail dress with a full ballerina skirt and a square neckline that softened her sharp collarbones. On the hanger, it didn't look like much, but on

Audrey, well, the dress seemed made for her. Givenchy was smitten. Thereafter, Audrey and Givenchy's relationship would become one of the longest-running fashion collaborations in history. Audrey often said the clothes he designed for her made her feel "protected."[2] Given her past, it is not hard to see why Audrey always wanted to feel safe.

Born in 1929, Audrey Kathleen Ruston spent her childhood moving between Belgium (her birthplace), England, and the Netherlands. When Audrey was six, she experienced what she later recalled as "the most traumatic event in my life"[3] when her father abandoned the family. According to Audrey, her mother's hair went white from shock and from then on Audrey felt the "constant fear of being left."[4]

That fear only grew stronger when, five years later, Germany invaded Holland. Audrey's childhood became a life of smoke-filled skies, bomb scares, and trucks carrying off Jewish friends to concentration camps, never to be seen again. At age thirteen, she witnessed her uncle and cousin being shot by German soldiers. Food became so scarce that Audrey was forced to eat tulip bulbs and cooked grass to stay alive.[5] One day, she found some bug-infested flour and recalled being overjoyed. The bugs meant she would finally have some protein.[6]

On May 5, 1945, the suffering came to an end when Holland was liberated on her sixteenth birthday.

Audrey never forgot the jubilant American soldiers who strode through the streets handing out chocolate bars. She devoured five bars in a matter of seconds and promptly got sick. (And so began her life-long love of chocolate.)[7]

After the war, she and her mother moved to London and Audrey studied ballet, practicing over four hours a day. Despite her hard work, Audrey was told she was too tall, too skinny, and far too old to ever become a prima ballerina.

Audrey fell to Plan B. She moved to the US and, despite her terrible stage fright, made it to the stage on Broadway and then began taking small movie roles. She played hotel receptionists, cigarette girls, and typists. These were not the smart, stylish roles that would turn her into a fashion icon, but they did keep her humble. When she later won an Academy Award for her role in *Roman Holiday*, she was so stunned she almost walked offstage instead of collecting her award. Audrey described her success as a "complete mystery" and confessed, "I never thought I was going to be an actress."[8]

She certainly was not your typical movie star, but what she did have was spunk. While buxom starlets posed like dolls on silk

Audrey adored hats of all shapes and sizes and wore everything from simple, elegant pillbox hats to outrageous, large-brimmed hats.

divans during photo shoots, Audrey came to life in front of the camera, turning barefoot cartwheels in the air and making funny faces. Nor was her thin frame the beauty ideal of the time. When studio executives asked her to pad her bra to look more curvaceous, she said no way. She would do it her way or not at all. Women across America fell in love with her lithe figure, prompting the director of *Sabrina*, Billy Wilder, to predict that Audrey would make "bosoms a thing of the past."[9]

She certainly didn't need a large bosom for her starring role in *Breakfast at Tiffany's*—the movie that would catapult her into the Fashion Hall of Fame. In it, she plays Holly Golightly, a society girl with a carefree spirit and a penchant for sparkly things. Audrey said it was the hardest role she ever played, probably because it was the biggest departure from her personality.[10] She was required to act saucy (she was shy), eat a Danish (she hated them), and hug a wet cat (the cat smelled awful). In a form-fitting black dress, oversized sunglasses, alligator shoes, and French twist hairdo, Audrey charmed audiences and the film became a smash. On set, her costars described her as a "cutup," always smiling.[11] Audrey took her work seriously, but never took herself too seriously.

Audrey once said, "My greatest ambition is to have a career without becoming a career woman."[12] She always put people first. She believed, "Giving is living. If you stop wanting to give, there's nothing more to live for."[13] In 1988, she traveled to Ethiopia, Somalia, and Sudan, serving as UNICEF Goodwill Ambassador.

She cradled sick children in her arms and gave speech after speech to raise money, declaring, "I will not rest until no child goes hungry."[14]

Audrey never stopped giving. And she did not live her life through the prism of fame. She once said, "If I blow my nose, it gets written all over the world. But the whole image people see of me is on the outside. Only we ourselves know what goes on; the rest is all in people's minds."[15] Whether she was in jeans and a T-shirt or a ladylike black dress, Audrey only cared what was on the inside. She will forever be a style icon, but it is her dignity, poise, and generosity of spirit that is most remembered as being so Audrey.

## AUDREY STYLE TIPS

1. **Forget trends.** Instead of buying a million pieces of trendy clothing, Audrey purchased a few quality items that would never go out of style. Save for a designer scarf, black ballet flats, or classic dress. Choose items that you know you will wear again and again.

2. **Act regal.** Audrey's ballet training and stern mother taught her to stand up straight and carry herself with grace and dignity. Practice your posture and wear a tiara for a dressy event to help you act the part.

3. **Use the power of simplicity.** Audrey never overdid accessories: long, white gloves and clip-on pearl-and-diamond-stud earrings added a touch of sophistication to her look. When not on set, Audrey was the most beautiful relaxing in her garden in jeans, a polo shirt, and clogs.

4. **Celebrate your assets.** Audrey hated her flat chest, crooked teeth, big feet, and the small bump in her nose. But instead of focusing on perceived flaws, she played up her assets: a belt cinched at her waist, sultry makeup to complement her eyes, and cropped hair to accent her cheekbones. Know your body and choose clothing and accessories that play up your best features.

5. **Focus on true beauty.** Audrey did not spend her days hobnobbing at Hollywood parties with celebrity attention seekers. She rolled up her sleeves and traveled the world helping others. To Audrey, kindness was the truest form of beauty.

# TRY A CLASSIC AUDREY HEPBURN FRENCH TWIST

**Tools**

- Rattail comb
- Hair clips
- Hairpins
- Bobby pins
- Hair spray

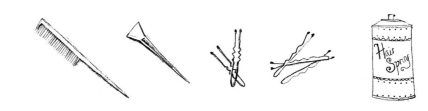

**Step 1.** With a rattail comb, divide hair horizontally across head from ear to ear into a front and back section. Clip the front section out of the way.

**Step 2.** Cross the back section of hair over to the left side and use bobby pins to clip the hair up the center. (Tip: Crisscross the bobby pins for a more secure hold.)

**Step 3.** Brush the back section of hair to the right and then twist the hair under your finger to form a barrel toward the head as you move upwards. Combine extra hair with hair from Step 1.

**Step 4.** Secure the twist with hairpins as you move up the back of the head.

**Step 5.** Divide the front section into a big section and a small section. Clip the smaller section closer to the forehead to keep it out of the way.

**Step 6.** Roll the larger hair section into a barrel toward the front of the head and secure it with hairpins along the base.

**Step 7.** Release the front hair. Divide it into two sections.

**Step 8.** Take the left section and wrap it around the back of the twist. Hold it in place with hairpins. Repeat for the right section. Finish with hair spray.

*Tip: If your hair is shorter, use a foam hair donut (see illustration) cut in two to bulk up the volume of the barrel.*

*Tip: Add a tiara at the base of the barrel or a rhinestone tennis bracelet secured with bobby pins.*

# Audrey Hepburn Style

Updo

Ballet flats

Long gloves

Black turtleneck

Chocolate

Black eyeliner

Pixie crop

Thick brows

Nude makeup

"I believe in pink"

Tiara

False eyelashes

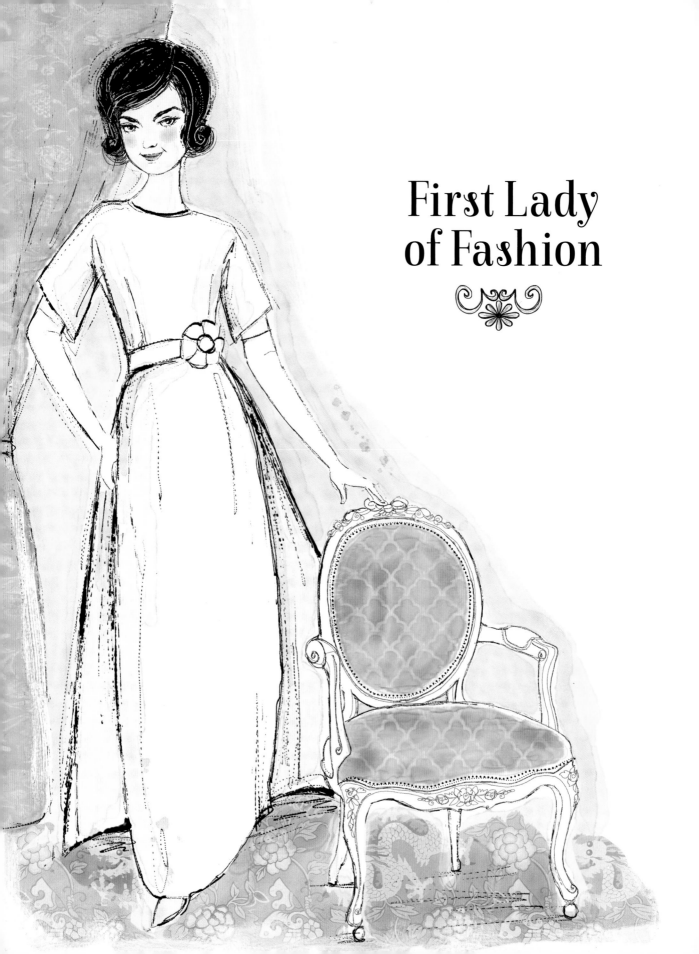

# First Lady
# of Fashion

# JACQUELINE KENNEDY ONASSIS
## 1929–1994

*She did it in her own way, and on her own terms,*
*and we all feel lucky for that.*

JOHN F. KENNEDY, JR.

First Lady. Jackie hated that silly title. She thought it made her sound like a "saddle horse."[1] Jacqueline (pronounced Jack-a-LEAN) Lee Bouvier Kennedy was not about to be a trained pony, but she was savvy enough to know that a president's wife had to play her part and that meant dressing with grace and style.

Let's start with what she is most remembered for: the pillbox hat. In the 1960s, respectable ladies never left the house without wearing a hat. (It would be like leaving the house today without underwear.) Most 1960s hats had large rims, demure veils, and wedding cake concoctions of flowers and feathers. Just like any accessory, the right hat could make or break an outfit. Jackie had one problem; she hated hats. And she had a good reason, as she had a rather humongous head for someone her size. So when she stuck a large hat on her large head . . . well, she looked a bit like a bobblehead doll or a bigheaded, cartoon character. It wasn't pretty.

Enter the pillbox hat—a small hat with a flat crown that made Jackie's big head look smaller. Pillbox hats were worn before Jackie in the 1950s but had never caught on. All of that changed on President John F. Kennedy's inauguration day on January 20, 1961. Jackie took her first steps into the White House wearing a fawn-colored wool coat with a matching pillbox hat. Unfortunately, it was also an extremely windy day. When she got out of the car, she put her hand to her hat and dented it.[2] That dent appeared in all the photographs. A fashion catastrophe? Not a chance.

American women just assumed that Jackie's hat was dented on purpose. Women ran out to buy pillbox hats and dented them to match Jackie's damaged hat. Soon, designers were denting their pillbox hats to appeal to the new trend. Jackie just had that effect on people. She could make even a wardrobe malfunction look stylish.

Oddly, the Kennedys never predicted that Jackie's fashion sense would be loved by so many women. In fact, they worried the American public would view Jackie as a complete snob. She wore designer clothes and a trendy, bouffant hairdo. She spoke French, and spent her free time at foxhunts and fancy dinner parties. The typical suburban housewife couldn't possibly relate to this aristocratic debutante.

But they did. To start, she brought impeccable manners to the White House. She learned the customs of visiting diplomats, knew every staffer's name, and always sent personal thank-you cards out within a day of receiving a gift. She dressed elegantly and confidently: sleek A-line shifts, large sunglasses, low-heeled pumps, and goddess-like pastel evening gowns.

Bringing prestige to the White House was not exactly an easy task. Before Jackie, the White House was a bit of an embarrassment and was even referred to as the "public shabby house."[3] With her usual irreverent wit, Jackie called it, "a wholesale furniture store during a January clearance."[4] The great staterooms were decorated with gaudy vintage replicas, paint was peeling off the walls, rugs were faded, and the floors

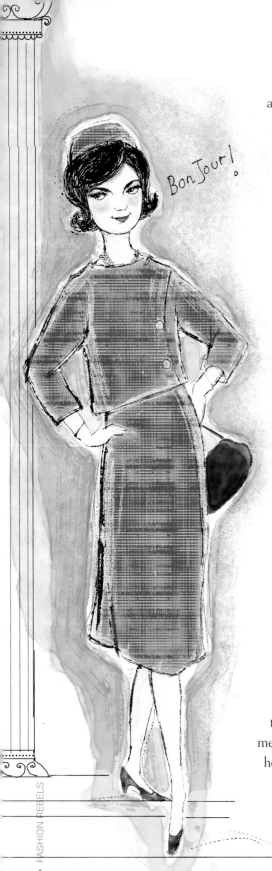

Bon Jour!

of the Oval Office were covered with cheap, brown linoleum. There were few bookcases, antiques, and very little charm. The White House needed a serious makeover.

In the past, a president's family could help themselves to anything in the White House when they left. That meant some of the historical furniture, paintings, rugs, and extremely valuable décor left with each president. So Jackie successfully advocated for a new law that forbade anyone from taking anything out of the White House.[5] She then established the White House Fine Arts Committee to "restore" (she hated the word redecorate) some of White House's original furniture. Jackie explained, "These things are not just furniture. They're history."[6] She set out to bring the White House back to its former glory, choosing the year 1802, the year the White House was built, as her inspiration. She said, "If we don't care about our past, we can't have very much hope for our future."[7]

Those hopes were dashed on November 22, 1963, at a campaign stop in Dallas, Texas. President Kennedy had asked Jackie to accompany him, and, for the first time, Jack also asked Jackie what she intended to wear. She modeled several outfits, but Jack thought she looked "smashing" in a Chanel knock-off. It was made out of a soft, pink wool with clean lines, a navy collar, navy trim, and of course, a matching pillbox hat. Little did she know that simple, pink suit would be forever associated with tragedy.

The day was bright and sunny. The kind of day where smiles are not forced and waves look natural. The couple was in a Lincoln convertible with the top down making their way slowly down Elm Street. Enthusiastic admirers lined the streets as the couple passed the Texas School Book Depository Building. Suddenly, shots rang out. The crowd erupted in panic. An assassin named Lee Harvey Oswald was later believed to have fired the shot that killed the president.[8]

While the nation mourned the loss of their leader, Jackie reminded the public, "There will be great presidents again, but there will never be another Camelot (a romantic reference to the legendary court of King Arthur.)[9] To make her husband's legacy endure like the great Arthurian tales, Jackie insisted that his funeral end with her lighting an "eternal flame" to keep "something living."[10] Jackie understood the power of symbols. She knew the nation needed a symbol for that which could never die—hope. History could be rewritten or forgotten, but hope would burn brightly for generations to come.

Jackie later remarried and retreated into private life, becoming a highly respected book editor. Her sunglasses got larger and she wore more black (which made it harder for the paparazzi to take her picture.)

# Jacqueline Kennedy Onassis Style

Envelope clutch

Pillbox hat

Pearls

Low-heeled pump

A-line sheath

Big sunglasses

Enamel jewelry

White kid gloves

Colors

# SKIRTING AROUND FASHION

The skirt is the second oldest garment in history (the loin cloth is the first). Both men and women have worn it, and its shape has changed more than any other garment in history.

In the **fourteenth century** (the Middle Ages), European women wore long, heavy skirts that fell to the ground, while men wore short skirts that allowed them to ride horses, hunt, and move easily.

206 BCE–589 CE, wealthy Chinese women wore a long, loose, multicolored skirt tied at the waist. It was so long that it had to be carried by servants so that the hem would not get dirty.

In the **sixteenth century,** the farthingale kept women fashionable but made moving around difficult. Worn by Queen Elizabeth I, the farthingale was a hooped skirt stiffened with ropes, whalebone, or wire and could be as large as five feet wide. To accommodate the wider skirts, doorframes had to be enlarged.

2600–1400 BCE, the Minoans on the island of Crete (now Greece) wore a bell-shaped, A-line skirt with flouncing ruffles over metal or wood hoops.

In the **seventeenth and eighteenth centuries,** panniers enlarged hips while keeping the front and back flat. Panniers, meaning "basket," were made of wood, metal, reeds, or whalebone. Marie Antoinette resented being stuffed into panniers and favored looser fitting gowns.

In **1856,** the word "skirt" became slang for women and the caged crinoline swept across Europe and America. Made of steel and worn under stiffened petticoats, one bad gust of wind could send fashionistas tumbling around like an inside-out umbrella.

In **1889,** an ankle-length skirt fitted below the knees or at the ankles, called the hobble skirt, wrapped up women's legs and continued to prevent them from taking any big strides toward fashion liberation.

In **1864,** the bustle put the focus on a woman's derriere and made women resemble snails. Made of cushion pads or frames of wood and wire, the bustle restricted women to a six-inch stride and made sitting difficult.

SKIRTING AROUND FASHION •

101

In **1941,** in the midst of WWII, American women were asked to "make do and mend" as wartime rationing controlled the amounts of buttons, pleats, and fabric that could be used in skirts. A very boxy skirt, called a utility skirt, became the uniform of patriotic gals.

In the **1950s,** fashion got high-school spirit as circle skirts became the staple item with young American girls. A circle skirt required as much as eleven yards of fabric and had to be dried over an umbrella to keep its shape. The most popular circle skirt was the poodle skirt, distinguished by its felt material and the appliquéd poodle at the bottom.

In **1921,** American women got the right to vote and hemlines rose. Drop-waisted, pleated skirts allowed women called "flappers" to finally climb stairs without taking baby steps. Suddenly, showing a bit of shin became the "bee's knees" as women like Josephine Baker shimmied across Europe and America.

In the **1960s,** the race for which country would be the first to walk on the moon began and American women took a "giant leap" in the shortest skirt in history— the miniskirt. Some shorter miniskirts ended as far as six inches above the knee.

In the **1970s,** inspired by Middle Eastern fashions, the hippie skirt or "broomstick skirt" was worn by freedom-loving American girls. It looked very similar to what the ancient Minoans wore.

In the **1980s,** fashion starlets like Madonna wore poofy ball gowns in tiers of lace.

**Today,** fashion runways all over the world display every type of skirt, from maxi, midi, mini, to flare or fitted. Choose your style or choose a different one every day.

Seriously . . .
Don't Take Yourself
Too Seriously

# ELLEN DEGENERES
## BORN 1958

*For me, the most important thing in your life is to live your life*
*with integrity, and not to give in to peer pressure.*

ELLEN DEGENERES

The camera zooms in on Ellen's face for her latest CoverGirl commercial. She flashes a severe scowl and a model-worthy pout. You might think she is about to explain how she got such porcelain skin and eyelashes like a baby giraffe, until she narrows her gray eyes and says, "Some models look so maaaaad."[1] She strikes a few dramatic poses, throws one shoulder back, and declares; "Maybe it's that they spend too much on department store makeup."[2] That may be one reason, but the real reason might be that they do something Ellen never does—take fashion too seriously.

The comedian and talk show host simply doesn't believe in judging others. She never looks in magnification mirrors, hates those obnoxious fashion "dos and don'ts," and advises us, "Accept who you are. Unless you are a serial killer."[3] Ellen makes being yourself look as "easy, breezy" as her commercials. But the truth behind those hip vests and laid back Converse sneakers is that while she has always accepted herself, she fought a long, hard battle to get others to accept her back.

Ellen Lee DeGeneres was born in a suburb outside of New Orleans on January 26, 1958. When she was thirteen, she learned the power of laughter after her parents divorced. When her mother Betty would get depressed, Ellen would cheer her up with punchy jokes.

She once told her mom, "I thought I should write you a letter," and sent her a handwritten letter containing only a big "P."[4] After high school she began doing standup comedy in local New Orleans clubs. While other comedians poked fun at people for their race, beliefs, or gender, Ellen just told grandma jokes. Ellen believes, "There's enough fear and negativity in the world without adding to it."[5]

She was finally discovered in Los Angeles when a booking agent from the *Tonight Show*, then hosted by the legendary Johnny Carson, caught her act at the Hollywood Improv Comedy Club. After a comedian did their segment, Carson would invite the best acts up for a one-on-one interview. That night, Ellen became the first female comedian ever asked by Carson to join him on the couch. She later referred to the outfit she wore for that television appearance as, "a tablecloth type shirt with huge pants" and joked she was taking "fashion advice from Sinbad."[6]

In 1994, she landed the leading role in the sitcom *Ellen*, where she played a neurotic bookstore owner who struggles with her identity. Never one to fear boundaries, she shocked her audience when she confessed to forty-two million viewers that she was gay.[7] It was the first time a woman had come out on primetime television. The resulting backlash was initially catastrophic for Ellen's career. Even though she had received four Emmy nominations and three Golden Globes for her role, her show was cancelled a year later. Magazines and late night talk shows threw their share of mean girl punches, with headlines like, "Yep, she is too gay."[8] Televangelist Jerry Falwell called her "Ellen Degenerate"—a rather juvenile attack that Ellen later worked into one of her acts. For three years after coming out, the phone didn't ring and Ellen couldn't get a job. She went through a period where she described herself as "furious" at the world, but she learned to ask herself "Who are you without fame?"[9]

So, Ellen went back to square one, doing what she loved most—standup comedy. Her act remained clean and she continued to deliver smart jokes. Her unique approach won her the role as the voice of Dory in Pixar's 2003 animated film *Finding Nemo*—a part that was written specifically for her. In the movie, Dory is a loveable blue tang fish that advises her discouraged friend Marlin to "Just keep swimming, just keep swimming, just keep swimming." It's advice Ellen obviously followed. Three years later, she was offered to host her own talk show, the *Ellen DeGeneres Show*.

Ellen has gone on to win thirty-six Daytime Emmy Awards for her show, written three bestselling books, started her own record company, become the spokesmodel for CoverGirl cosmetics, and done a stint as an American Idol judge (she hated being mean to people). In 2015, she launched her own retail brand, E.D., that includes everything from fashion apparel to house and pet wares. She has also hosted the Emmys and the Academy Awards, proving she has come a long way from taking fashion advice from Sinbad. For the 2007 Academy Awards, she dressed in typical unpretentious Ellen style—a Gucci, maroon velvet suit with a white blouse. That was her serious look. For the 2001 Emmys, she was more playful in a white, feathered skirt with a stuffed swan wrapped around her neck—a nod to the infamous swan dress singer Björk wore for the Academy Awards earlier that year. At the 2014 Oscars, she wore a midnight-blue velvet suit for her opening monologue and then changed into a tailored white suit for the now-famous star-studded selfie. (The uploaded photo crashed Twitter.)

Ellen's talk show continues to be one of the top-rated daytime shows. She always wears clothes she can dance in, usually a stylish blazer, vest, pants, and Keds. With so much color in her personality, Ellen usually sticks to neutral colors—white, gray, black, and navy. Sometimes she adds a little whimsy with a striped tie, polka-dot socks, or brightly colored belt.

Despite being in the spotlight, Ellen DeGeneres is an uncooperative trendsetter. In interviews, she admits to being an introvert who hates small talk and doesn't like to be the center of the attention. When asked in one interview why she is so popular, Ellen modestly replied, "It beats me."[10] When asked about regrets, Ellen confesses she is happy she lost so much after her first show was canceled because it taught her how to let go and realize that not everyone was going to like her.[11]

Wherever she goes, Ellen dresses to please one person: herself. That means comfort always comes first. In 2006, she demonstrated her love of comfort clothes during a surprise appearance at the Tulane University commencement. While most guest speakers would be dressed to impress, Ellen wore a white terry-cloth bathrobe and fuzzy slippers. As

she looked around dumbfounded at the graduates in starched caps and gowns she explained, "They told me everyone would be wearing robes."[13]

During that commencement speech she also offered these words of wisdom, "Never follow anyone else's path, unless you're in the woods and you're lost and you see a path. Then by all means you should follow that."[14] Like any good comedian, there is always some truth in her jests. Her style may be playful, preppy, and sometimes silly, but her honesty keeps her on the right path.

## ELLEN'S STYLE TIPS

1. **Floss every day.** Ellen believes flossing is the key to good health. She might be onto something there. Missing teeth is never a good look on anyone.

2. **Be nice to people.** Ellen always gives her guests thoughtful (and often humorous) gifts. She never says bad things about other stars and always ends every show with "be kind to one another."

3. **Drink lots of water.** Ellen has great skin. It must be the water.

4. **Dance. Laugh. Play.** If you Google images of Ellen, you will have a hard time finding her without a big grin (unless she is mockingly making a serious face). Her fashions match her playfulness. If a dress or shirt doesn't make you feel like dancing around the room, don't buy it.

# HOW TO ROCK A TIE LIKE ELLEN

The half-Windsor knot and Windsor knot are named after the Duke of Windsor—a man who was always sharply dressed. Fortunately, you don't have to own a castle to look as debonair. This activity is for a half-Windsor knot because it is easier to learn than the Windsor knot and it works on lighter fabrics.

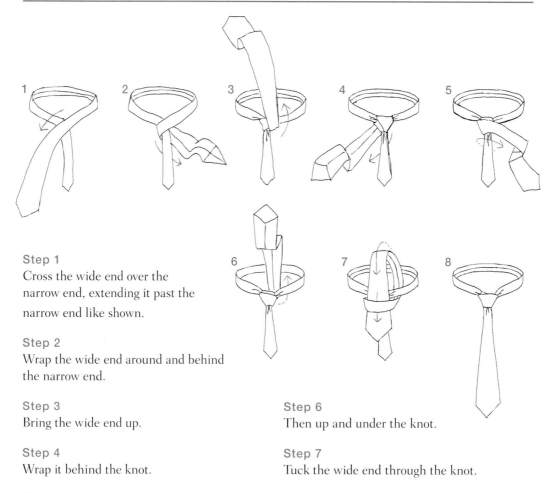

**Step 1**
Cross the wide end over the narrow end, extending it past the narrow end like shown.

**Step 2**
Wrap the wide end around and behind the narrow end.

**Step 3**
Bring the wide end up.

**Step 4**
Wrap it behind the knot.

**Step 5**
Wrap the wide end across and in front of the knot.

**Step 6**
Then up and under the knot.

**Step 7**
Tuck the wide end through the knot.

**Step 8**
Pull to desired tightness.

# Ellen DeGeneres Style

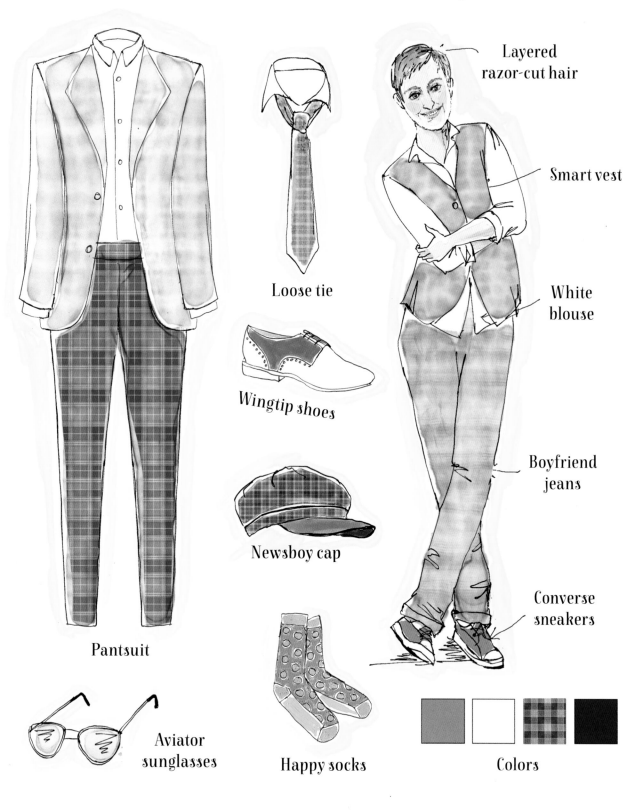

Loose tie

Wingtip shoes

Newsboy cap

Pantsuit

Aviator sunglasses

Happy socks

Layered razor-cut hair

Smart vest

White blouse

Boyfriend jeans

Converse sneakers

Colors

The
Phoenix of
Fashion

# MADONNA
## BORN 1958

*It all has to do with an attitude and loving yourself the way you are.*
MADONNA

Singer, songwriter, dancer, actress, mother, philanthropist, author, entrepreneur, fashion icon. Defiant, brave, egotistical, talented, contradictory, loyal, always changing, never stagnant. Trying to contain Madonna is like trying to contain a flame in a sealed jar. If you put a lid on it, you are left with ashes. But unlike other super talents that burn bright only to eventually burn out, Madonna has risen from her ashes over and over again, each time reborn in a style more original than the last.

Madonna has kept her fans and "wannabes" on a dizzying chase to keep up with her style reinventions. She is still remembered for her punk rock style that had eighties teens tying tights in their streaky hair like head-wound patients and wearing enough silver crucifixes and rosaries to ward off vampires. Then she morphed into a bargain-basement bride with tulle skirts, fingerless white lace gloves, dark lipstick, and bushy eyebrows. So many teens copied Madonna's look that Macy's opened "Madonnaland"—an entire department store filled with day-glo bras, lace leggings, black tube skirts, and thrift-store-chic jewelry.

But just when her fans might have pegged her as a troublemaking street urchin caught in an exploding closet of accessories, she dramatically streamlined her style with platinum blonde hair pulled back into a slick ponytail and one dangerously pointy cone bra. Then just as easily she sloughed off the hard shell like a molting snake and softened her look with sophisticated Marilyn Monroe curls and retro 1950s dresses. Madonna explains her philosophy on change as "No matter who you are, no matter what you did, no matter where you've come from, you can always change, become a better version of yourself."[1]

Madonna Louise Veronica Ciccone was born on August 16, 1958, in Bay City, Michigan. Her father was a first generation Italian American and the only one in his immediate family to go to college. He worked as an engineer in the defense industry while Madonna's mother (also named Madonna) was an X-ray technician. That job as an X-ray technician may have led to the breast cancer that took Madonna's mother away from her when she was just six years old.[2] Madonna would later say of her mother's death, "You walk around with a big hole inside you, a feeling of emptiness and longing . . . and I think a lot of times that's why you become an overachiever."[3] Madonna channeled the loss of her mother into an insatiable desire to stand out. To show her individuality at her high school talent show, she wore a bikini and covered herself in fluorescent body paint—an outfit that horrified her very Catholic father. (She was grounded for two weeks.)[4] But while most girls wanted to be the cutesy cheerleader, Madonna cut her hair short, wore combat boots, and didn't shave her legs or armpits. She also started a punishing schedule of daily three-hour ballet lessons. For practices, she showed up in ripped leotards held together by safety pins and wore black rubber band bracelets. (They were actually typewriter drive bands.)[5] But despite

her edgy appearance, she was not one of those kids loitering in the parking lot. She was a straight-A student who graduated a semester early and was more likely to munch on carrots sticks at a party than drink beer.

Her discipline paid off when she was awarded a scholarship to the University of Michigan. But other opportunities beckoned. In 1977, her sophomore year, she won a scholarship to study with the Alvin Ailey American Dance Theatre and moved to New York City to follow her dream of becoming a dancer.[6]

To make ends meet she took odd jobs—an artist's model, a coat-check girl in the famous Russian Tea room, and a server at Dunkin' Donuts. (She was fired after she squeezed jelly filling on a rude customer.)[7] At the time, all she could afford was a fourth floor apartment with nonstop noise, no elevator, and a few cockroaches scattering across the floor for company. A few cockroaches couldn't scare off Madonna. Although she had no formal training, she began to pursue a career as a singer and got more involved with New York's downtown music scene. Eventually, she scored a gig as the drummer in a rock band called the Breakfast Club.

Although being a drummer allowed Madonna to express herself musically, being in the background was never going to be her thing. So she quit the drumming gig and formed the rock group Emmy, with her as the lead vocalist.* After Emmy disbanded, her first big break came when she approached DJ Mark Karmins at a New York club and asked him to play her solo song, "Everybody." Karmins played the song the following night and the crowd loved it. They loved it so much that Karmins passed her name on to Sire Records, who signed her first solo song. That big break later led to a record deal and in 1984, she sang her first hit single, "Holiday," on American Bandstand. When the host Dick Clark asked Madonna what her dreams were for the future, she replied, "To rule the world."[8]

Madonna certainly has gone on to rule the world. She has created hit record after hit record and along the way written a bestselling children's

---

*You can still hear some of these original tracks on YouTube.

book series, won a Golden Globe award for best actress for the movie *Evita*, and become a mother to four children (two biological, two adopted). In 2006, she cofounded the nonprofit charity organization Raising Malawi, dedicated to providing better education and living standards to the children of Malawi. Feminist writer Camille Paglia says of Madonna's enduring legacy, "She shows girls how to be attractive, sensual, energetic, ambitious, aggressive, and funny—all at the same time."[9]

Madonna's fashion sense has influenced some of today's most popular pop stars. Lady Gaga paid tribute to Madonna's 1980s style by cropping her blonde hair and wearing studded leather jackets with heavy gold jewelry in her video for "Edge of Glory."[10] Singer Rihanna has said that she wants to be the "Black Madonna"[11] and when singer Gwen Stefani was accused of copying Madonna she replied, "show me one girl my age who was not influenced by her."[12] Rick Florino from Artist Direct has summed up Madonna's impact as a fashion leader; "Her influence is everywhere, and she's not going anywhere either."[13]

Today you just never know how she might show up on the red carpet—as a dark haired avenging angel in a fairy tale dress or a blonde bombshell with gold encased teeth. Madonna certainly knows how to keep her audience guessing. Her style choices tell a dramatic story in many acts—from scrappy ruffian clawing her way up the pop charts to sophisticated mother and philanthropist. Always changing. Never boring. Each look more different than the last.

# Madonna Eighties Style

Hair bow

Cross earrings

Dishwater blonde

Blue eyeshadow

Red lips

Tiered lace skirt

Jelly bracelets

Fingerless lace gloves

Layered necklace

Leg warmers

Cropped jean vest

Neon colors

# Homegrown Style

# MICHELLE OBAMA
## BORN 1964

*[Michelle] wears both high fashion and low fashion—*
*it's modern, democratic, and, above all, American.*
ANDREW BOLTON, CURATOR, THE COSTUME INSTITUTE

It began with a fist bump. Just a casual hand gesture between Michelle Obama and her husband Barack after he won the 2008 Democratic presidential nomination. It was a natural gesture to match her commanding outfit: a silk crepe sheath dress in a bright, majestic purple paired with a studded leather belt, gumball-sized pearls, and (gasp!) no stockings. Michelle's outfit was admired for its bold color and clean lines, but the knuckle rapping gesture caused some controversy. Critics found it too aggressive. Supporters found it endearing. One thing is for certain: as soon as Michelle Obama went knuckle to knuckle with her toned biceps flexing, the nation knew Mrs. O was not your demure wallflower.

She certainly has not dressed like previous First Ladies. She has dared to show her buff arms in A-line sheaths and bold patterns. She doesn't wear panty hose because she finds them "painful" and defended her choice to go barelegged with a simple "It feels better."[1] Most importantly, she has shown that you can look elegant without an extravagant clothing budget. Although she occasionally wears haute couture clothing for special events, she has also appeared on *The Tonight Show* wearing J.Crew cardigans and pencil skirts. For her appearance on *The View*, she wore a $148 sleeveless sheath with a graphic black-and-white leaf print from retailer White House Black Market. Within forty-eight hours, the dress sold out. Much like Marie Antoinette (see page 24) and her carefree *gaulle*, women across America could now look as comfortable and as stylish as the First Lady.

It's easy to understand Michelle's unpretentious style choices given her humble background. Michelle Robinson Obama was born on January 17, 1964, and grew up in a one-bedroom apartment on Chicago's tough South Side. Her father worked as a pump operator in a water plant while her mother stayed home to care for Michelle and her brother Craig. As a kid, Michelle was no slacker. She was so smart that she skipped the second grade, always made honor roll, and was a member of the National Honor Society. After high school she was accepted to Princeton University and went on to Harvard Law School. She got her first job at Chicago law firm, Sidley & Austin, where a young, up-and-coming intern named Barack Obama was assigned to her.

When Michelle first met Barack she was not impressed.[2] He was wearing an ugly sports jacket and, even worse, had a cigarette hanging out of his mouth. But despite the poor first impression, Barack charmed Michelle. (He eventually quit smoking when he took office in 2008.) After they were married and had two children, Barack decided to run for president. Michelle quit her job to help him campaign and has been by his side ever since looking poised and powerful.

Michelle's signature style is mostly sleeveless sheaths or fit-and-flare dresses with high-waisted belts to accent her tall stature. Her unfussy style has been a refreshing change from the usual power suits and stiffly coiffed hair of recent First Ladies. She has become the epitome of "high-low style"—pairing affordable outfits from J.Crew, the Gap, and H&M with fashion accessories from high-end design-ers or an antique brooch from her personal collection. Michelle has

Designer Christian Dior has called purple, "the king of colors."[3] Michelle often wore purple while on the campaign trail.

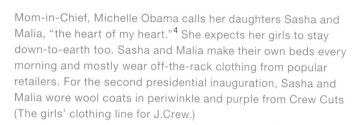

Mom-in-Chief, Michelle Obama calls her daughters Sasha and Malia, "the heart of my heart."[4] She expects her girls to stay down-to-earth too. Sasha and Malia make their own beds every morning and mostly wear off-the-rack clothing from popular retailers. For the second presidential inauguration, Sasha and Malia wore wool coats in periwinkle and purple from Crew Cuts (The girls' clothing line for J.Crew.)

shown that she can buy any common retail dress and make it her own.

When asked about her fashion sense she has said, "It's fun to look pretty."[5] Michelle certainly knows how to have fun. For many White House events, she has kicked off her shoes and run barefoot across the lawn and hula hooped in comfortable capri pants. In fact, it is hard to get a picture of Michelle standing still. She wakes up at 5:00 AM every morning to work out with her husband before dropping the kids off at school.[6] She has also made it her mission to whip the rest of America into shape. To get kids eating healthier, she has got her hands dirty alongside Washington DC elementary students and planted homegrown food in the White House kitchen garden. Coolest of all, she has danced at events across the country for her Let's Move campaign to get kids exercising. (And yes, the First Lady can really move.)

If fashion is a way to communicate, Michelle has kept the conversation real. She describes her personality as having "no surprises."[7] She says, "I don't want to be anyone but Michelle Obama. And I want people to know what they're getting."[8] In affordable sundresses and flats, she is just like every other busy mom, juggling getting the kids to soccer practice while keeping up with her passions. Of course, not every soccer mom has her style choices so closely scrutinized. When asked on *The View* why the media is so obsessed with what she wears,

Michelle dismisses the attention with her usual nonchalant response, "I fill up some space."[9]

Michelle's dry understatement goes part and parcel with her cool sense of style, and she walks the talk. In the past, the White House staff was never allowed to show skin. Even in the sweltering heat of DC, women's arms had to be covered and legs had to be stuffed into pantyhose. Michelle changed all that. The Washington bureau chief for *People* magazine, Sandra Sobieraj Westfall, believes the First Lady has "redefined the standard of what is professional and what is acceptable, and we women get to enjoy more options."[10] In carefree cardigans and sleeveless sheaths, Mrs. O has fist bumped her way uptown, downtown, and into the hearts of fashion lovers.

# Michelle Obama Style

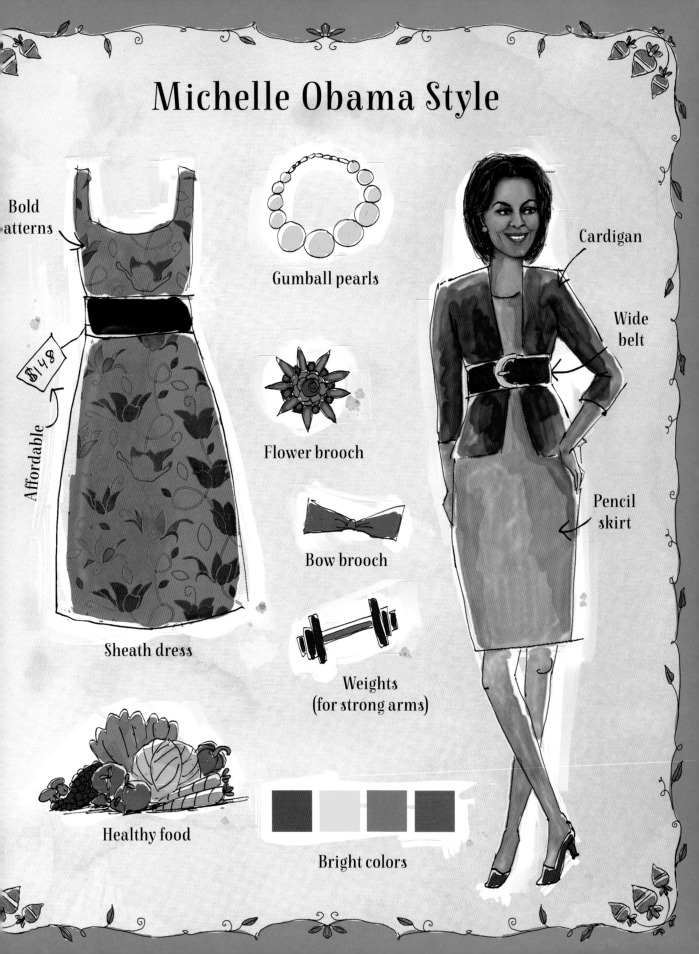

Bold patterns

Gumball pearls

Cardigan

Wide belt

Flower brooch

Bow brooch

Pencil skirt

$148

Affordable

Weights (for strong arms)

Sheath dress

Healthy food

Bright colors

# FIRST LADIES OF FASHION

Throughout history, First Ladies have set trends and become symbols of American style. Here are a few of the most memorable First Ladies and the fashions they loved.

### MARTHA WASHINGTON
### 1731–1802
You might think of Martha as that old lady in paintings in her white kerchief and cap, but Miss Martha had some moxie in her younger days. She loved clothes but chose to dress conservatively to show she understood everyday Americans. She wore frugal, homespun dresses, often recycled from silk stockings.

### DOLLEY MADISON
### 1768–1849
Dolley always turned heads in her plunging necklines and feathered turbans. At her parties she kept a parrot on her shoulder and a smile for every guest. She was the first First Lady to strike a balance between looking regal and democratic.

### JULIA TYLER
### 1820–1889
Julia never shied away from the spotlight. While other First Ladies avoided the press, Julia befriended reporters and became the first First Lady to pose for a new technology—photography. She kept an exotic Italian greyhound by her side and for formal occasions dressed in white satin ball gowns with a diamond ferronnière (a fancy way of saying headband) in her hair.

### HARRIET LANE JOHNSTON
### 1830–1903
Even with the Civil War on every American's minds, no one could stop talking about James Buchanan's niece Harriet (who was her bachelor uncle's First Lady) and her plunging bertha collar necklines (an off-the-shoulder, V-shaped neckline). Her philanthropic causes were as popular as her fashions. She founded the Harriet Lane Home for Invalid Children, which is now part of Johns Hopkins Children's Center in Baltimore, Maryland.

### MARY LINCOLN
### 1818–1882
Mary could have been a fashion icon if it had not been for a real buzz kill called the Civil War. Mary didn't quite get that looking glitzy while most people in the country are poverty stricken is a big fashion no-no. She wore huge ball gowns of expensive silks and was often criticized for her shopping sprees.

### FRANCES CLEVELAND
### 1864–1947
Frances, or "Frankie," as she was called by the press, was the first First Lady to become an advertising icon. Her image was slapped on everything from soaps and perfumes to biscuit tins and liver pills. Women across America copied her bustled dresses and hair styled in a bun "à la Cleveland."

### GRACE COOLIDGE
#### 1879–1957

In the roaring twenties, women could finally vote, and wearing pants and playing sports had become acceptable. Always on the move, Grace embraced all these radical new trends by wearing sleeveless red flapper dresses and posing for pictures with her pet raccoon.

### ELEANOR ROOSEVELT
#### 1884–1962

Eleanor didn't care much for extravagance (unless it was a fabulous hat). As First Lady, Eleanor wore five dollar off-the-rack dresses to demonstrate that she was sensitive to the poverty most women encountered during the Great Depression. Working class girls followed her example and wore simple cotton dresses.

### MAMIE EISENHOWER
#### 1896–1979

Mamie was all about pink, pink, and more pink. She wore so much bubblegum pink that the color became known as "Mamie Pink." She was also known for girly off-the-shoulder dresses, baby bangs, fur stoles, and mail-ordered hats in—you guessed it—pink.

### JACQUELINE KENNEDY
### 1929–1994

It's easy to be trendy; just follow the masses. It's another thing to have style. Style is timeless. Jackie not only brought style and sophistication to the White House, she also made it look effortless. Her simple A-line dresses, pearl necklaces, and oversized sunglasses are still the epitome of chic fashion.

### NANCY REAGAN
### 1921–2016

The 1980s was a decade of power suits, shoulder pads, and high-waisted jeans. Nancy finessed that trend by balancing femininity with strength in ladylike white gloves, column dresses, or tailored suits in bold crimson, dubbed "Reagan Red."

### MICHELLE OBAMA
### BORN 1964

Michelle knows fashion doesn't have to cost a fortune. She is known for combining statement designer pieces with off-the-rack clothing from popular retail stores. Whether she is hugging Queen Elizabeth II in a cardigan or jumping rope in shorts, Michelle's style is all about keeping it real.

Born This Way

# LADY GAGA
## BORN 1986

*I want people to walk around delusional about how great
they can be, and then to fight so hard for it every day
that the lie becomes the truth.*

LADY GAGA

Set against the space age theme song from Alfred Hitchcock's movie *Vertigo*, an alien creature emerges from a slime-encased pod. She's wrapped in a glittering rhinestone top and her hair is styled high in a Marie Antoinette pouf. Sharp mountain peaks of skin jut out from her forehead and there is some sort of freaky third eyeball stuck to her chin. The camera zooms in on her black, kohl-rimmed eyes as she states in a monotone, "This is the manifesto of Mother Monster."[1]

Like most of Lady Gaga's music videos, the imagery for "Born this Way" does not lend itself to easy interpretation. When asked about the meaning behind her "manifesto," Lady Gaga replies that she imagines another world with, "a new race—a race within the race of humanity, a race that bears no prejudice."[2]

Her fashions are out of this world too. From disco ball bras to dresses of draped raw meat, Miss Gaga's traffic-stopping fashions have become an endless source of entertainment for comedians and late-night hosts. But Gaga may be having the last laugh: she is the first artist to pass the four million mark in digital sales,[3] and fans (her "Little Monsters") can't get enough of her quirky style.

Born Stefani Joanne Angelina Germanotta, Gaga's childhood was not marked by drama. She grew up on the affluent Upper West Side of Manhattan and attended the Convent of the Sacred Heart School—an all-girl school where socialites such as Paris and Nicky Hilton have paraded the halls.

Despite her privileged upbringing, Gaga still felt like an outcast. The other kids called her "rabbit teeth" because of her big teeth and, according to Gaga, "I got made fun of."[4] It didn't help that she also did not dress like the other girls. She styled her hair in Marilyn Monroe curls and dressed in bright vintage Thierry Mugler suits with huge shoulders and cinched waists[5]—not exactly your usual modest convent girl school attire.

At seventeen, she enrolled in New York University's Tisch School of the Arts but dropped out her sophomore year to pursue music. That's when her dad made a deal with her. He would pay her rent for one year as long as she promised to go back to school if she had not made it by the end of the year.[6] Determined to make her dreams

Today, Gaga has an image-making team of young fashion designers and art directors (all under 26) for her "Haus of Gaga."

happen, Gaga hopped from club to club, playing the piano and singing her heart out. She then met producer Rob Fusari who came up with the name Lady Gaga as homage to the Queen song "Radio GaGa."[7]*

As the newly created Lady Gaga, her first style choices were a mishmash of eighties go-go costumes with a masculine edge: punkish leotards, jackets with big shoulders, and fishnet stockings with sky-high heels. She hardly ever wore pants. (Gaga claims she doesn't wear pants because her partially blind grandmother has an easier time making out her shape on stage with bare legs.)[8]

*Accounts differ on the origins of the name. In several interviews, Gaga has claimed that she came up with the name after Fusari said she was so "Radio Gaga."

By 2007, she had kept her promise to her father and was signed to Interscope Records. In 2008, she released her first solo album, *The Fame*, and tore up the pop charts with hits like "Just Dance," "Poker Face," and "Paparazzi." The album earned a Grammy for Best Electronic/Dance Album, which she accepted wearing a short silver dress with a lightning-bolt hat. It looked like it might hurt someone.

Not a lot of fashion statements can take out an eye but Lady Gaga has that effect. She has worn bras that shoot fire, corsets with silver futuristic sculptures, and sunglasses made from razor blades. While other pop stars exist in a 2D space of glossy magazine covers, Gaga slices into a 3D space where fashion becomes an art form that begs to be viewed from all sides. Take for example the dress covered with Kermit the Frogs as a statement against wearing fur. Then there was the bubble-making machine dress that made real bubbles. And let's not forget that she met Queen Elizabeth II of England wearing a red latex number with full Elizabethan-style sleeves. (The queen ate it up.) She has worn Christmas trees in her hair, tall crowns, and sculpted her hair into a giant bow. Gaga fashion is not for the timid.

Would any of it be described as pretty? That's probably not what Gaga is after. To start, she has never tried to change her face through plastic surgery even though many pop stars

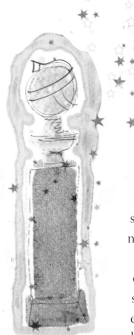

Gaga's star continues to rise. In 2016, she won a Golden Globe for Best Actress for her role in *American Horror Story: Hotel.*

have gone under the knife. In fact, sometimes she doesn't even show her face, often performing in a full mask. The masks are certainly dramatic, but they also serve another purpose. With her features hidden, Gaga seems to be asking her audience to see her as an artist and not as an object of beauty. Or so we can guess.

Whatever her meaning, Gaga has become the odd bird in the red carpet parade of pretty starlets flashing their plumage. She can't even be put on any "Worst-Dressed" list because her fashion choices don't always resemble actual garments. (Does a bubble-making machine count as a dress?) But maybe that is the point. When asked to describe her style philosophy, she says, "When I say to you there is nobody like me, and there never was, that is a statement I want every woman to feel and make about themselves."[9] Gaga probably does not expect her fans to dress like a pant-less alien, but she does want them to have the courage to embrace their inner misfit. Or at the very least . . . be comfortable being born that way.

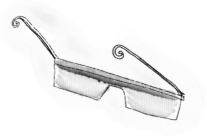

# HOW TO ADD GAGA GLAM TO YOUR SHOES

### Supplies

- Shoes that need some glam
- Fabric glue
- Rhinestones
- Paintbrush
- Lace

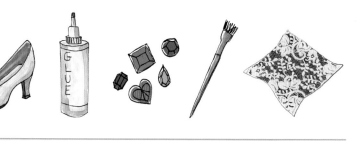

### Step 1

Clean the surface of the shoes and stuff newspaper inside to protect them. If dampened, let them dry completely.

### Step 2

Spread fabric glue over shoes with a paintbrush.

### Step 3

Wrap lace over the entire shoe, making sure to leave extra lace hanging over the sole.

### Step 4

Cut the lace down the middle and trim it to 1/8 inch around the edge. Fold the 1/8-inch hem down and glue it to the inside of the shoe.

### Tip

*To add a bit more bling, glue embellishments to the top of the shoes. Try some old earrings (try breaking off wire posts), bows, rhinestones, flowers, metal spikes, or some vinyl material cut into a star.*

# Lady Gaga Style

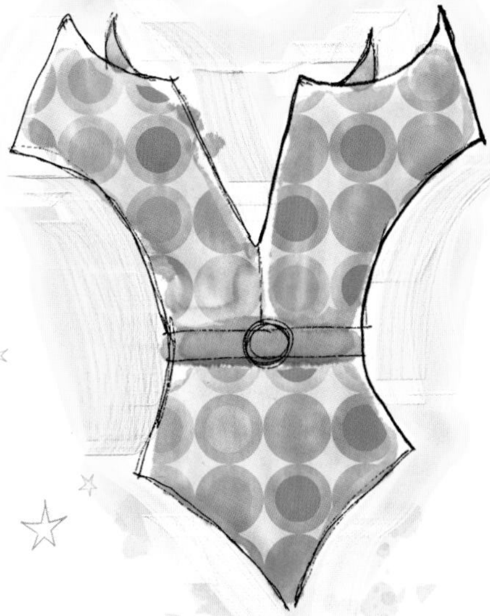

Hair bow

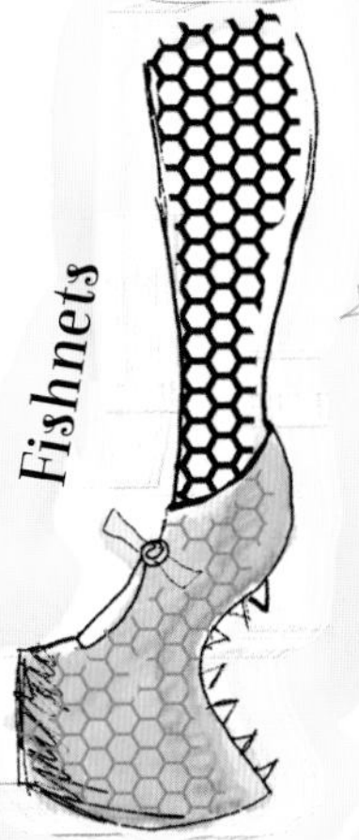

Fishnets

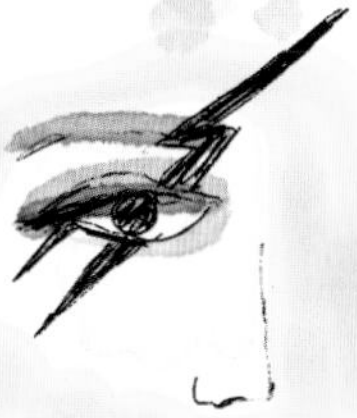

Leotard

Lightning bolt

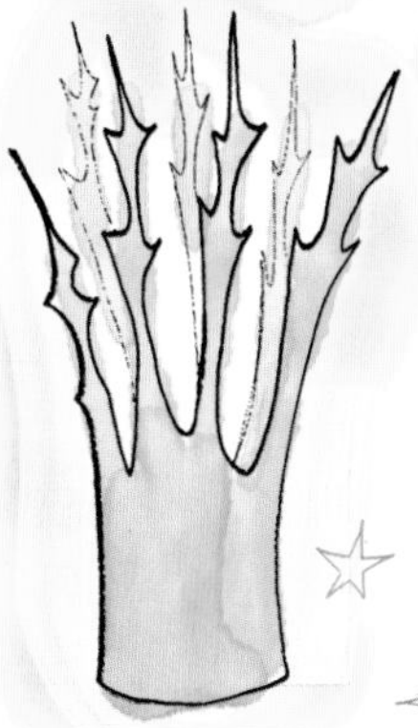

Crown

Shoulder pads

Mask

Sharp objects

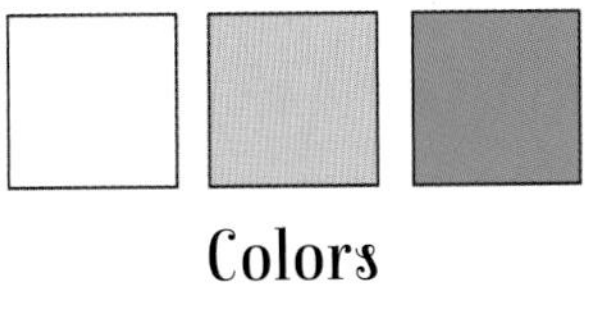

Colors

Disco ball dress

# The Many Faces
# of Michelle

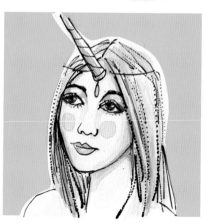

# MICHELLE PHAN

## BORN 1987

*Confidence is a personal journey.*

MICHELLE PHAN

When you first sit down to watch a Michelle Phan YouTube video tutorial, it's like stepping into a relaxing spa with your new best friend. Suddenly, scary things like tweezing your brows and "how to become more self-confident"[1] seem like a breeze. (Hint: The self-confidence part has nothing to do with the brows.) The next minute, Michelle's soft, silver-bell voice, tranquil doe-eyed gaze, and goofy "I am in this with you" sense of humor will have you cracking an egg on your face. (Check out her "Egg Mask Facial"[2] video. I promise it will make your skin glow.) So how did a child of poverty-stricken Vietnamese parents go from barely surviving on food stamps to building a fashion and cosmetics empire? Michelle credits her success to being an accidental entrepreneur, but with over seven million YouTube subscribers, a cosmetics line, her own production company, and a recent book, it's hard to give serendipity all the credit.

Michelle "Tuyet Bang" Phan was born on April 11, 1987, in Boston, Massachusetts. "Tuyet Bang" is her Vietnamese name meaning, "snow that has exploded" or "avalanche." Her father gave Michelle this name because a single snowflake is so delicate, but combine those snowflakes . . . and you have an "unstoppable force."[3] It has proven to be a fitting name for the unstoppable force that his daughter has become.

When Michelle was just three months old her family traveled cross-country to San Francisco, California, in a junky van that could barely start. Life was hard in California. Michelle constantly had to change schools because her family was always in debt. As a result, she made only one friend while she lived there. She did find comfort in drawing. She often did not have paper so she would draw on the extra pages at the back of phone books or, to her parents' chagrin, on the walls.[4]

Her family then moved to Tampa, Florida, where her dad struggled to find work. Hoping for better employment opportunities, her father moved back to Boston and promised he would return soon. Michelle had a feeling that he was not coming back. She promised her father, "If you leave us, I'll find you when I grow up."[5] However, it was her father who found her after she had become an internet sensation. He told Michelle that he had always known she would be okay in life.[6]

Michelle's mother later remarried, but Michelle did not get along with her stepdad. Life was tough in Tampa. Michelle's bed was a sleeping bag on the floor and the family's one-bedroom apartment had no furniture. There were also few Asians in her school and the mean girls taunted her with chants of "Ching chong."[7]

To try to fit in, Michelle would try different looks— tanned skin to look more Hispanic or braids to look more African American. She admits that she was trying on different looks to "hide the true me."[8]

Today, she tries different looks "to celebrate different facets" of herself and her life.[9] As a self-taught makeup artist and self-professed "digital nerd,"[10] Michelle takes an artistic approach to cosmetics and fashion. She uses her face and body like a canvas that she constantly wipes clean and repaints. Her first video in 2007 was a tutorial on natural-looking makeup. Other videos followed, offering simple but useful advice on everything from how to dress up jeans to how to stretch your too-small shoes with ice. From there she went on to more theatrical demos—how to look like K-pop star, a Cyber Gothic Anime character, or even your favorite Disney Princess. Much like creating your own fantasy avatar, Phan has morphed her face into everything from a terrifying "Zombie Ghoul," to a tantalizing "Egyptian Queen." After your tenth or so video (they are mildly addictive) you start to realize makeup is so much more fun when it is less about looking pretty and more about playing with beauty ideals.

Michelle's big breakthrough came when a Lancôme executive watched one of her videos on "Airplane Beauty Tips."[11] (Michelle recommends collagen masks to stay hydrated, even though it might weird out the person next to you on the plane.) At the time, Lancôme was spending thousands of dollars on slick cosmetic tutorials and not getting anywhere near the views that Michelle was getting for her quirky homemade videos. They offered Michelle a job as their official, "video makeup artist" and flew her to Paris and New York.[12] Michelle soon started her production company, "FAWN" (For All Women Network), and she launched Em, an affordable makeup line backed by L'Oréal.

Michelle knows how to have fun with different styles, but she is always careful to point out to her viewers that even models and movie stars don't have perfect bodies or perfect skin, but do have perfectly applied makeup and even more perfect lighting.

It's a lot of success for someone so young, but Phan is a natural teacher. Her videos have smart and simple instructions paired with just the right amount of charm and silliness to keep her from coming off like a robot. She doesn't blather on and on in her videos like some YouTube presenters, and she doesn't do haul videos (where she reviews everything she's purchased online). Since Michelle came from a world of "have-nots" she is very careful to make her videos more about having fun with fashion and not about having stuff. She believes the fashion choices we make tell a story.[13]

Whether she is an Egyptian Queen or a K-pop star, Michelle inspires her fans to experiment, have fun, and (if you screw up), crack an egg on your face and see if you don't glow.

Despite all her fame, Michelle still edits all her own videos. And, believe it or not, she says she rarely wears makeup in daily life.

# Michelle Phan Style

Romantic *or* Rock Star

Rose necklace

Layered skirt

Pale lipstick

Nude eyeshadow

Classic bag

Spiked headband

Plaid skirt

Black lipstick

Platform bootie

Black eyeliner

Old Soul,
Young Heart

Love, ☆
☆Tavi

# TAVI GEVINSON
## BORN 1996

*I think that people admire people that look weird and dress interestingly or whatever because they wish that they could be that courageous.*

TAVI GEVINSON

How old is Tavi Gevinson? It's the first question that comes to mind for most people. At just eleven years old, she created the blog *Style Rookie*, a fashion site with rather humble beginnings. *Style Rookie* didn't use professional models. Instead, Tavi posed for the camera wearing her favorite outfits in front of a makeshift tripod in her yard.[1]

Her look was hard to pin down. Tavi's wide-set eyes, doll-like thick bangs, icy glare, and translucent skin made her appear like a child vampire who would never age. She paired that delicate ingénue with floral granny dresses, pillbox hats, chunky knitted scarves, orthopedic-looking saddle shoes, and oversized blazers that swallowed her four-foot-ten frame. I've got to be honest. If you were dressed by your colorblind, eccentric, bargain-shopping grandmother, you might end up looking a little like Tavi's first fashion statements. It's this ironic juxtaposition of childlike innocence and crazy old lady style that confused most people. It also led to the same questions over and over again: How did she get the chutzpa to dress like that, followed by . . . And how old is this girl?

The answer to the second question doesn't really matter as much these days to the writer, editor, public speaker, singer, and actress. Tavi Gevinson was raised in Oak Park, Illinois, and graduated from Oak Park and River Forest High School. She began her blog in sixth grade partly because she was "extremely bored"[2] and partly because she felt if she dressed completely different then she wouldn't be compared to anyone else.[3]

It worked. Tavi's style choices put her in a class of her own. Those first fashion shoots were a jumbled mess of vintage dresses paired with artsy accents—thick glasses, flowers in her hair (à la Frida Kahlo), and Joni Mitchell-inspired bangs (1970s music icon and one of her fashion idols). What Tavi most liked about fashion was that is was "never just about fashion" because it was "connected to everything else."[4] With this more conscious approach, she pulled fashion inspiration from an eclectic mix of favorite books, Greek Mythology, art history, her mood boards, or simply what was on her iPod playlist. In one interview, she assembled a tiara made from plastic houses and paper flowers.[5] Fashion for Tavi was never about looking pretty. It was her ultimate artistic expression.

That honest self-expression caused her blog readership to grow to thirty thousand readers a day and it wasn't long before big name designers were inviting Tavi to fashion week. Japanese designer Rei Kawakubo had her flown to Tokyo for a holiday shindig and she hung out with the creative director of the House of Chanel, Karl Lagerfeld. Eventually she came to the attention of the editor-in-chief of *Sassy* magazine, Jane Pratt, who suggested that Tavi start her own magazine and offered to help her. Tavi met with her to brainstorm creative ideas and from those first brainstorming sessions, *Rookie* magazine was born.[6]

Tavi admits that *Rookie* "doesn't have all the answers"[7] but knows, "If an article we put up can make one person feel better about themselves, then that's good enough for me."[8] Tavi feels that teens are far more multi-dimensional than they are portrayed in the media and she feels it is her mission to better represent real teens. Those are the kind of girls that want to read articles like "How to Look Like You Weren't Just Crying in Less Than Five Minutes"[9] and are less concerned with the size of their butts and more concerned with "Farting and Getting Away with It."[10]

You would expect nothing less from a self-professed "pop culture nerd."[11] In one interview, Tavi wore an eyeball necklace while cracking sardonic jokes about whom she murdered for the eyeballs. Her advice to get your body back in time for the school year is simple; two slices of pizza, a glass of soda, and, um . . . mixed greens with a healthy portion of ranch dressing. She's kidding. Sort of. Just like her quirky fashion tastes, Tavi has that kind of off-kilter, subversive humor that might make some people uncomfortable.

After graduating from high school, Tavi moved to New York City where she cut those snarky teeth on the acting world. In 2014, she starred in the Broadway performance of *This Is Our Youth* where she played a perceptive fashion student named Jessica Goldman—one of a trio of wayward teens struggling to find herself in 1980s New York City. *Newsweek* described her performance as, "simply delightful"[12] while the *New Yorker* described her as a "star being shaped by her own will."[13]

Tavi is definitely shaping her destiny. Where will it take her next? As far as fashion goes, it is low on her list of priorities and her style reflects that shift. Gone are the eyeball necklaces, hodgepodge collage of granny dresses, and homemade tiaras. Instead, you will find her dressed more like a typical New Yorker in a minimalistic black dress and chin-length, cropped hair. And as far as those

1 THE HEAD.

Fig. 1.

crazy old lady fashion statements, Tavi admits that she has no regrets about her earlier style choices. She says, "even if I see an old photo of myself and know that I wouldn't wear that now, I'm glad I gave myself permission at that time to go for it because it made me more confident and it was just really fun."[14]

Tavi speaks to her readers as if she is the fun big sister who tells you how it is or the best friend that never judges. Tavi is not the popular girl. She's a misfit who fits her every fashion choice. Still, Tavi never tells girls that feeling confident is going to be easy. She muses, "The idea that feeling confident and feeling misunderstood are mutually exclusive really bugs me."[15] It's that kind  of wisdom that makes you forget just for a moment that Tavi Gevinson is only a teenager. At the very least, she's a wise, old soul trapped in a teenager's body.

# Tavi Gevinson Style

Granny sweater

Thick-rimmed glasses

Flowers in hair

Collared blouse

Star tiara

Eyeball necklace

Patterned skirt

Butterflies

Journaling

Knee highs

Colors

Daisies

Guitar

# The New Fashionista
# Hall of Fame

Even more so today, fashion is always in a perpetual state of change. The following young icons are not only keeping up, but also shaking up the fashion world.

# BETHANY MOTA

With millions of YouTube subscribers, a spot on Dancing with the Stars, and her own clothing line, it's hard to believe Bethany Mota ever sat alone at her school's lunch table. A target of bullying when she was thirteen, Bethany channeled her pain into creating soft-spoken haul videos on makeup and fashion.[1] Since then, her confidence and her fans (called *Motavators*) have grown and she has created hundreds of videos on everything from making DIY healthy popsicles, marbled nail art, and crop tops, to the importance of being kind to one another.

## Bethany's Style
Bethany's style is a cross between bubbly and bohemian. She loves girly stuff like bows and flowers but is still low-maintenance enough to kick back in Keds and a T-shirt.

Bows

Military boots

Owl purse

Flower dress

*"All makeovers should be about enhancing who you are."*[2]

# MARY KATE AND ASHLEY OLSEN

Big sunglasses

Big bags

Leather pants

Maxi dresses

First off, don't call them the Olsen twins because they are not joined at the hip. However, they are joined when it comes to growing their impressive fashion empire. Aside from reaching billionaire status, in 2012 the Olsens won *Womenswear*'s Designer of the Year, even beating out superstar Marc Jacobs. The sisters began their rise to fame on the sitcom *Full House* when they were just nine-month-old babies wearing nothing but diapers and blonde topknots. As they grew, so did their teen fans who were desperate to copy anything they wore.

With naturally visionary eyes for fashion, the sisters' three clothing lines—The Row, Elizabeth and James, and Olsenboye—always seem one year ahead of the trends.

## Mary Kate and Ashley's Style

The Olsen's have mastered high/low fashion—combining minimalistic, affordable clothing with statement pieces. (Think simple, one-color dress from Target with splurge-worthy drop earrings.) And although the two may be small in stature (Mary Kate is five foot two, Ashley is five foot three), they are not afraid to make large style statements: oversized glasses, big slouchy bags, and long maxi dresses.

# VENUS AND SERENA WILLIAMS

Sibling rivalry can sometimes be a bad thing—unless it drives two sisters to tennis stardom and a fashion empire. Serena Williams has won over thirty Grand Slam Titles and four Olympic gold medals. Her sister Venus has won more than twenty Grand Slam titles and four Olympic gold medals. Venus credits her don't-settle-for-less attitude to her parents who never allowed her to come home with Cs in school. Serena believes that her success is partly due to not worrying about what other people think or trying to be part of the "in crowd."[3] Off the court, Venus has a successful fashion line called EleVen and Serena's is called Aneres.

Beaded braids

Tennis racquet

Wild patterned tennis dress

## Venus and Serena's Style

The sisters design mostly activewear apparel in hard-to-miss floral patterns, bold geometric prints, and traffic-stopping color. With such dedication to pursuing dreams, the Williams sisters' clothing lines serve up a winning combination of style and comfort.

# ZOE DAMACELA

It's one thing to become a talented fashion designer. It's another thing to become a successful businesswoman too. Struggling with her single mom to make ends meet, and at one point even homeless, Zoe Damacela began her first business venture selling greeting cards door to door when she was just eight years old. At fourteen, she started her own apparel company and sold her first dress for an unprofitable thirteen dollars.[4] Since then, she has gone on to sell her collection of peplum dresses, smart jackets, and ruffled blouses around the world. She has met with President Obama, been on the cover of *Seventeen* magazine, and designed clothes for Macy's, all while attending Northwestern University. When asked what is the most important advice she can pass on to young entrepreneurs, Zoe says, "It's okay to fail."[5] And by fail she means, don't be afraid to walk away from a venture and start again and again until you get it right.

Ruffles

Peplum dress

Gathered waist dresses

## Zoe's Style

Zoe's style is all about attention to details. She designs dresses with an eye for how the dress moves—ruffles, princess seams, and gathered waists give her dresses structure. She also never forgets about little things like using a pretty fabric on the liner of a dress.

# BRITTNEY GRINER

At a towering six feet eight inches tall, it's not surprising that basketball star Brittney Griner was once called "freak" at school. Tired of the taunts, Brittney learned to fight back by becoming a dunking, dribbling, passing, blocking virtuoso . . . while wearing gender-bending suits and bow ties. By her senior year playing basketball for Baylor University, Brittney had scored 3,203 points and had blocked 736 shots—setting an NCAA record.[6] Today, the openly gay athlete has marked out her need for honest self-expression in tattoos, declaring, "It's my life. It's my skin. It's my ink."[7] In 2014, she switched to ink on paper to silence the haters. Her inspirational autobiography, *In My Skin*, is a must-read for any girl struggling to find her true self.

## Brittney's Style

Brittney is as fearless on the court as she is in fashion. The girl can rock a bow tie like nobody's business and often wears an eclectic mix of tailored suits and vests with pops of color and patterns. You might guess it is her ultracool black Vans that give her such a swagger, but it's more likely how she wears her undeniable confidence.

Basketball

Tattoos
(try temporary)

Vests

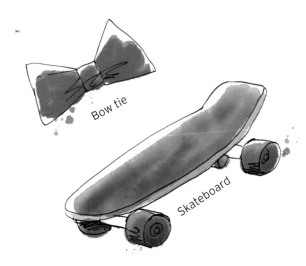

Bow tie

Skateboard

Vans

# Become Your Own Fashion Rebel

*Give a girl the right footwear and
she can rule the world.*

BETTE MILDER, ENTERTAINER

Every day, you wake up and go to your closet and make a very powerful choice—how do I want to communicate who I am to the world? And the best part about making that decision is the choices are limitless. Maybe you decide to be a ladylike Audrey Hepburn with a dash of Lady Gaga extreme. (Wearing ballet flats with Lady Gaga's infamous Kermit the Frog dress would make it far easier to get around.) Or maybe one day you feel showy and put flowers in your hair à la Frida Kahlo, but decide to pair it with some simple Ellen-inspired Converse. (Because you're not feeling *that* showy.) No matter what you decide to communicate, it's your choice. Fashion allows you to imagine the possibilities.

The women in this book blazed new trails in fashion by making style choices that stood for something. Coco Chanel envisioned a world where women dressed as comfortably as

men. Jacqueline Kennedy knew the power of symbols and created a magical aura of "Camelot" to illustrate American prestige. Josephine Baker certainly didn't let the haters hold her down because of the color of her skin. All that banana shaking represented one thing—freedom.

I hope you find inspiration in these ladies' style choices and use what you've discovered here to find your own style. Entertaining quiz aside, your fashion sense may be similar to Audrey, Marilyn, or Josephine, but those ladies are not you. *You* are you. And only you know what you stand for. So experiment, have fun, be brave, and always be a fashion rebel.

# Acknowledgments

A special thank you to my agent, Abigail Samoun, who used her tireless matchmaking skills to find the perfect publisher for this book. My gratitude goes out to the designers and editors of Beyond Words, especially Nicole Geiger, who acted as one part cheerleader, one part editing magician to bring out the best in my writing. This book would also not have been possible without the patient librarians of the Lynnfield Public Library who never questioned why I needed to take out thirty books at a time. I also would be remiss in not thanking my six-year-old son, John, who splashed and dripped paint to contribute many of the watercolor backgrounds in this book. And lastly to my fashion-loving daughter Charlotte, who inspired me every morning by pulling together some pretty wild outfits.

# Notes

## Why Fashion Matters

1. Ruth La Ferla, "At 90, Fashion's Latest Pop Star," *The New York Times*, August 23, 2011, http://www.nytimes.com/2011/08/25/fashion/iris-apfel-90-stylish-and-on-hsn-up-close.html.
2. Ellen DeGeneres, *Seriously . . . I'm Kidding* (New York: Grand Central Publishing, 2011), 5.
3. Dolin Bliss O'Shea, *Famous Frocks: The Little Black Dress* (San Francisco: Chronicle, 2014), 85.
4. Malcolm Chandler, ed., *European History*, Teach Yourself (Lincolnwood, IL: McGraw-Hill/Contemporary Publishing, 2001), 115.
5. Joan McMahon Flatt, *Powerful Political Women: Stirring Biographies of Some of History's Most Powerful Women* (Bloomington, IN: iUniverse, 2012), 15.
6. Ivy Nyayieka, "And We Deserve to Twinkle," *Huffington Post*, February 12 2014, http://www.huffingtonpost.com/ivy-nyayieka/and-we-deserve-to-twinkle_b_6657890.html.
7. Amy Alexander, *Fifty Black Women Who Changed America* (New York: Kensington, 2003), 87.

## Cleopatra VII

1. Stacy Schiff, *Cleopatra: A Life* (New York: Little, Brown and Company, 2010), 71.
2. Duane W. Roller, *Cleopatra: A Biography* (New York: Oxford University Press, 2010), 58.
3. Schiff, *Cleopatra*, 39.
4. Ibid., 16.
5. Ibid., 42–43.
6. Ibid., 70.
7. Diana Preston, *Cleopatra and Antony* (New York: Walker & Company, 2009), 76.
8. Ibid.

9. Roller, *Cleopatra*, 126.
10. Margaret Melanie Miles, *Cleopatra: A Sphinx Revisited* (Berkeley: University of California Press, 2011), 29.

## Elizabeth I

1. Alison Weir, *The Life of Elizabeth I* (New York: Ballantine Books, 1998), 13.
2. Ibid., 222.
3. Royal Museums Greenwich, "Body and Dress," *Royal Museums Greenwich*, www.rmg.co.uk/explore/sea-and-ships/in-depth/elizabeth/the-queen%27s-court/body-and-dress.
4. Victoria Sherrow, *Encyclopedia of Hair: A Cultural History* (Westport, CT: Greenwood Press, 2006), 399.
5. Janet Arnold, *Queen Elizabeth's Wardrobe Unlock'd: The Inventories of the Wardrobe of Robes Prepared in July 1600* (Oakville, CT: David Brown Book Co., 1988), 2.
6. Jane Ashelford, *Dress in the Age of Elizabeth I* (New York: Holmes & Meier, 1988), 141.
7. S. P. Cerasano and Marion Wynne-Davies, *Gloriana's Face: Women, Public and Private, in the English Renaissance* (Detroit, MI: Wayne State University Press, 1992), 69.
8. Sherrow, *Encyclopedia of Hair*, 115.

## Marie Antoinette

1. Tom Standage, *An Edible History of Humanity* (New York: Walker & Company, 2010), 119.
2. Stefan Zweig, *Marie Antoinette: The Portrait of an Average Woman* (New York: Grove Press, 2002), 96.
3. Caroline Weber, *Queen of Fashion: What Marie Antoinette Wore to the Revolution* (New York: Picador/Henry Holt, 2007), 107.
4. Zweig, *Marie Antoinette*, 97.
5. Weber, *Queen of Fashion*, 113.
6. Ibid., 162.
7. Ibid., 358.
8. Ibid., 158.
9. Ibid., 215.

## Dolley Madison

1. Catherine Allgor, *A Perfect Union: Dolley Madison and the Creation of the American Nation* (New York: Henry Holt, 2013), 3.
2. Ibid., 5.
3. Ronald Blumer, "A Politician's Wife," in "Dolley Madison," *American Experience*, directed by Muffie Meyer (Arlington, VA: PBS, 2010), DVD.
4. Mary Beth Norton, Jane Kamensky, Carol Sheriff, David W. Blight, and Howard Chudacoff, *A People and a Nation: A History of the United States*, 10th ed. (Independence, KY: Cengage Learning, 2014), 225.
5. Hugh Howard, *Mr. and Mrs. Madison's War: America's First Couple and the Second War of Independence* (New York: Bloomsbury Press, 2012), 53.
6. Molly Yun, "Ice Cream: An American Favorite Since the Founding Fathers," *PBS*, 25 July 2013, http://www.pbs.org/food/features/ice-cream-founding-fathers.
7. Allgor, *A Perfect Union*, 189.
8. Blumer, "Dolley's Political Performance," *in* "Dolley Madison," *American Experience*, DVD.
9. Allgor, *A Perfect Union*, 232.
10. Blumer, "A Symbol of the Republic," in "Dolley Madison," *American Experience*, DVD.
11. Allgor, *A Perfect Union*, 247.
12. Ibid., 245.

## Coco Chanel

1. Justine Picardie, *Coco Chanel: The Legend and the Life* (New York: HarperCollins/It Books, 2011), 20.
2. Marcel Haedrich, *Coco Chanel: Her Life, Her Secrets* (Boston: Little, Brown, 1972), 34.
3. Karen Karbo, *The Gospel According to Coco Chanel: Life Lessons from the World's Most Elegant Woman* (Augusta, GA: Skirt!, 2009), 34 and 94.
4. Lisa Chaney, *Coco Chanel: An Intimate Life* (New York: Viking, 2011), 25.
5. Karbo, *The Gospel According to Coco Chanel*, 105.
6. Coco Chanel, Chanel No. 5 advertisement, *New York Magazine*, October 25, 1993, 28.
7. Karbo, *The Gospel According to Coco Chanel*, 105.

## Anna May Wong

1. Anthony B. Chan, *Perpetually Cool: The Many Lives of Anna May Wong (1905–1961)*, (Lanham, MD: Scarecrow Press, 2003), 73.
2. Ibid.

3. Graham Hodges, *Anna May Wong: From Laundryman's Daughter to Hollywood Legend* (Hong Kong: Hong Kong University Press, 2012), 10.

4. Chan, *Perpetually Cool*, 17.

5. Hodges, *Anna May Wong*, 19.

6. Ibid., 21.

7. Ibid., 57.

8. Ibid., 181.

9. Shirley Jennifer Lim, *A Feeling of Belonging: Asian American Women's Public Culture, 1930–1960* (New York: NYU Press, 2005), 83.

10. Andrew Bolton, *China: Through the Looking Glass* (New Haven, CT: Metropolitan Museum of Art, 2015), 67.

11. Chan, *Perpetually Cool*, 33.

12. Hodges, *Anna May Wong*, 121.

13. Ibid., 136.

### Josephine Baker

1. Jean-Claude Baker and Chris Chase, *Josephine Baker: The Hungry Heart* (New York: Cooper Square Press, 2001), 144.

2. Ean Wood, *The Josephine Baker Story* (London: Sanctuary Publishing, 2000), 33.

3. Margot Ford McMillen and Heather Roberson, *Into the Spotlight: Four Missouri Women* (Columbia, MO: University of Missouri Press, 2004), 63.

4. McMillen and Roberson, *Into the Spotlight*, 64.

5. Harper Barnes, *Never Been a Time: The 1917 Race Riot That Sparked the Civil Rights Movement* (New York: Walker & Company, 2008), 144.

6. Wood, *The Josephine Baker Story*, 27.

7. Baker and Chase, *Josephine Baker: The Hungry Heart*, 57.

8. Lesley M. M. Blume, "How Josephine Baker Helped Save Post-War French Fashion," *The Huffington Post*, June 7, 2010, http://www.huffingtonpost.com/lesley-m-m-blume/josephine-baker-fashion-h_b_601072.html.

9. Wood, *The Josephine Baker Story*, 155.

10. Schroeder and Wagner, *Josephine Baker*, 41.

11. Wood, *The Josephine Baker Story*, 205.

12. Schroeder and Wagner, *Josephine Baker*, 53.

13. Bennetta Jules-Rosette, *Josephine Baker in Art and Life: The Icon and the Image* (Champaign, IL: University of Illinois Press, 2007), 148.

14. Baker and Chase, *Josephine Baker*, 170.

15. Schroeder and Wagner, *Josephine Baker*, 53.

16. Baker and Chase, *Josephine Baker*, 235.

17. "La Baker Is Back," *Life Magazine*, April 2, 1951, Vol. 30, No. 14, 60.

18. Jules-Rosette, *Josephine Baker in Art and Life*, 13.

19. Ibid., 54.

20. Amy Alexander, *Fifty Black Women Who Changed America* (New York: Kensington Publishing, 2003), 86.

21. McMillen and Roberson, *Into the Spotlight*, 77.

## Katharine Hepburn

1. Karen Karbo, *How to Hepburn: Lessons on Living from Kate the Great* (New York: Bloomsbury, 2007), 13.

2. William J. Mann, *Kate: The Woman Who Was Hepburn* (New York: Henry, 2013), 37.

3. Katharine Hepburn, *Me* (New York: Knopf, 2011), 32.

4. Karbo, *How to Hepburn*, 32.

5. Jean Druesedow and Kohle Yohannon, *Katharine Hepburn: Rebel Chic* (New York: Skira Rizzoli, 2012), 55.

6. Ibid., 22.

7. Ibid., 65.

8. Karbo, *How to Hepburn*, 76.

9. Druesedow and Yohannon, *Katharine Hepburn*, 22.

10. Barbara Leaming, *Katharine Hepburn* (New York: Limelight Editions, 2000), 385.

11. Druesedow and Yohannon, *Katharine Hepburn*, 21.

## Who Wore the Pants?

1. Caroline Weber, *Queen of Fashion: What Marie Antoinette Wore to the Revolution* (New York: Picador/Henry Holt, 2007), 85.

2. Dexter C. Bloomer, *Life and Writings of Amelia Bloomer* (Boston: Arena, 1895), 80.

## Frida Kahlo

1. Amy Stechler, "Chapter 13," *The Life and Times of Frida Kahlo*, directed by Amy Stechler (Arlington, VA: PBS, 2005), DVD.
2. Andrea Kettenmann, *Frida Kahlo, 1907–1954: Pain and Passion* (Los Angeles: Taschen, 2007), 24.
3. Stechler, "Chapter 13," *The Life and Times of Frida Kahlo*, PBS.
4. Kettenmann, *Frida Kahlo, 1907–1954*, 10.
5. Hayden Herrera, *Frida: A Biography of Frida Kahlo* (London: Bloomsbury. 2003), 50.
6. John Morrison and Jamie Pietras, *Frida Kahlo* (Philadelphia: Chelsea House Publishers, 2003), 9.
7. Kettenmann, *Frida Kahlo, 1907–1954*, 18.
8. Stechler, "Chapter 2," *The Life and Times of Frida Kahlo*, PBS.
9. Helga Prignitz-Poda, Ingried Brugger, Peter von Becker, and Cristina Kahlo, *Frida Kahlo: Retrospective* (New York: Prestel, 2010), 139.
10. Emma Carlson Berne, *Frida Kahlo: Mexican Artist* (Edina: ABDO Publishing, 2010), 28.
11. Carlos Fuentes, *The Diary of Frida Kahlo, An Intimate Self-Portrait* (New York: Abrams, 2005), 211.
12. Christina Burrus. *Discoveries: Frida Kahlo, Painting Her Own Reality* (New York: Abrams, 2008), 70.
13. Kettenmann, *Frida Kahlo, 1907–1954*, 52.
14. Martha Zamor, *Frida Kahlo: The Brush of Anguish* (San Francisco: Chronicle Books, 1990), 56.
15. Morrison, *Frida Kahlo*, 87.
16. Fuentes, *The Diary of Frida Kahlo*, 272.

## Marilyn Monroe

1. Christopher Nickens and George Zeno, *Marilyn in Fashion: The Enduring Influence of Marilyn Monroe* (Philadelphia: Running Press Book Publishing, 2012), 16.
2. Ibid, 153.
3. Randy J. Taraborrelli, *The Secret Life of Marilyn Monroe* (New York: Grand Central Publishing, 2009), 161.
4. Paula Munier, *On Being Blonde: Wit and Wisdom from the World's Most Infamous Blondes* (British Columbia, Canada: Fair Winds Press, 2004), 54.
5. Taraborrelli, *The Secret Life of Marilyn Monroe*, 283.
6. Clark Kidder, *Marilyn Monroe: Cover to Cover* (Iola, WI: Krause Publications, 2003), 162.

7. Andrew Hansford and Karen Homer, *Dressing Marilyn: How a Hollywood Icon Was Styled by William Travilla* (London: Goodman, 2011), 96.

8. Keith Badman, *Marilyn Monroe: The Final Years* (New York: Thomas Dunne Books /St. Martin's Press, 2012), 157.

9. Ibid., 120.

10. Donald Spoto, *Marilyn Monroe: The Biography* (New York: Cooper Square Press, 2001), 165.

11. "I Dress for Men Says Marilyn Monroe," *Movieland Magazine*, July 1952, transcribed by Anastasia Takueva, http://www.marilynmonroe.ca/camera/mags/movieland.htm.

12. Nickens and Zeno, *Marilyn in Fashion*, 178.

13. "The Marilyn Tapes," *48 Hours*, produced by Nancy Kramer, Taigi Smith, Chris Young, April 20, 2006, New York: CBS, http://www.cbsnews.com/news/the -marilyn-tapes.

14. Taraborrelli, *The Secret Life of Marilyn Monroe*, 301.

15. Ibid., 309.

16. Nickens and Zeno, *Marilyn in Fashion*, 194.

17. Ibid.

## Audrey Hepburn

1. Pamela Clarke Keogh and Hubert de Givenchy, *Audrey Style* (London: Aurum, 2009), 22.

2. Diana Maychick, *Audrey Hepburn: An Intimate Portrait* (New York: Citadel, 1996), 231.

3. Donald Spoto, *Enchantment: The Life of Audrey Hepburn* (New York: Harmony Books, 2006), 14.

4. Ibid., 15.

5. Ibid., 30.

6. Maychick, *Audrey Hepburn*, 43.

7. Sean Hepburn Ferrer, *Audrey Hepburn, An Elegant Spirit* (New York: Atria Books, 2005), 47.

8. Melissa Hellstern, *How to Be Lovely: The Audrey Hepburn Way of Life* (New York: Dutton, 2004), 29.

9. Tony Nourmand, *Audrey Hepburn: The Paramount Years* (San Francisco: Chronicle Books, 2007), 90.

10. Barry Paris, *Audrey Hepburn* (New York: Berkeley Books, 2001), 173.

11. Ibid., 356.

12. Hellstern, *How to Be Lovely*, 45.

13. Spoto, *Enchantment*, 306.

14. Maychick, *Audrey Hepburn*, 233.

15. Hellstern, *How to Be Lovely*, 16.

## Jacqueline Kennedy Onassis

1. Donald Spoto, *Jacqueline Bouvier Kennedy Onassis: A Life* (New York: St. Martin's Paperbacks, 2000), 173.

2. Ellen Ladowsky, *Jacqueline Kennedy Onassis* (New York: Random House, 1997), 83.

3. Sally Bedell Smith, *Grace and Power: The Private World of the Kennedy White House* (New York: Random House, 2004), 253.

4. Spoto, *Jacqueline Bouvier Kennedy Onassis*, 236.

5. Public Law No. 87-286, 75 Stat. 586, September 22, 1961, www.gpo.gov/fdsys/pkg /STATUTE-75/pdf/STATUTE-75-Pg586-2.pdf.

6. Barbara Leaming, *Mrs. Kennedy: The Missing History of the Kennedy Years* (New York: Free Press, 2002), 49.

7. Tina Santi Flaherty, *What Jackie Taught Us: Lessons from the Remarkable Life of Jacqueline Kennedy Onassis* (New York: Perigee Books, 2014), 149.

8. "Chapter 2" of the "Warren Commission/Report of the President's Commission on the Assassination of President Kennedy," *National Archives*, 1964, www.archives.gov /research/jfk/warren-commission-report/chapter-2.html.

9. Randy J. Taraborrelli, *After Camelot: A Personal History of the Kennedy Family—1968 to the Present* (New York: Grand Central Publishing, 2013), XVIII.

10. Vincent Bugliosi, *Reclaiming History: The Assassination of President John F. Kennedy* (New York: Norton, 2007), 313.

## Ellen DeGeneres

1. "CoverGirl Simply Ageless—Ellen DeGeneres—Why So Mad?" *Adstorical*, http:// www.adstorical.com/commercial/2527/covergirl-simply-ageless-ellen-degeneres -why-so-mad.

2. Ibid.

3. Ellen DeGeneres, *Seriously... I'm Kidding* (New York: Grand Central Publishing, 2011), 9.

4. "Ellen DeGeneres," *Bio*, A&E Television Networks, accessed August 3, 2015, www .biography.com/people/ellen-degeneres-9542420/videos/ellen-degeneres-full-episode -2244678863.

5. Sharon Waxman, "Ellen DeGeneres Is Chosen as Host of Next Year's Oscars," *New York Times*, September 9, 2006, www.nytimes.com/2006/09/09/movies/09elle.html.

6. "Ellen DeGeneres: The Kennedy Center Mark Twain Prize," *PBS.org*, Aired October 24, 201, video.pbs.org/video/2296659257.

7. Lisa Iannucci, *Ellen DeGeneres: A Biography* (Westport, CT: Greenwood Press, 2009), foreword, x.

8. Tom Jicha, "DeGeneres' Courage Changes to Whining," *Sun Sentinel*, May 9, 1998, articles .sun-sentinel.com/1998-05-09/lifestyle /9805080279_1_ellen-degeneres-abc-s-lack-show.

9. "Ellen DeGeneres and Tracy Grimshaw—*A Current Affair* Interview," *YouTube*, 17:30, posted by "jayness33," February 27, 2013, https://www.youtube.com/watch ?v=FqK1-BfFEJw.

10. "Ellen DeGeneres Today Show Interview (Ellen talks about humor, happiness, & Jesus)," *YouTube*, 7:07, posted by "Videos about/with Ellen DeGeneres & Portia De Rossi," March 13, 2012, https://www.youtube.com/watch ?v=EhhE6KG-gxU.

11. "Ellen DeGeneres and Tracy Grimshaw, *YouTube*, February 27, 2013.

12. Ellen DeGeneres, *The Funny Thing Is . . .* (New York: Simon and Schuster, 2003), 4.

13. "Lend Me Your Beers: The Definition of Success Changes," *Elle*, slide 2 of 15, www.elle.com/pop-culture /celebrities/lend-me-your-beers -655791-2#slide-2.

14. "Ellen DeGeneres University Commencement Address (2009 Speech to College Students)," *YouTube*, 16:50. Posted by "The Book Archive." May 10, 2013, https://www.youtube.com/watch ?v=glauQaj0x6I.

## Madonna

1. Carol Benson & Allan Metz, *The Madonna Companion: Two Decades of Commentary*, The Companion Series (Independence, KY: Schirmer Trade Books, 2000), 42.

2. Carol Gnojewski, *Madonna: Express Yourself* (Berkeley Heights: Enslow Publishers, 2007), 25.

3. "Madonna: A Star with Staying Power," *CNN*, accessed May 24, 2014, www.cnn .com/CNN/Programs/people/shows/madonna/profile.html.

4. Andrew Morton, *Madonna* (New York: St. Martin's Press, 2002), 65.

5. Ibid., 139.

6. Ibid., 85.

7. Ibid., 74.

8. "American Bandstand Interview with Dick Clark." *YouTube*, 1:52, aired 1984, posted by "Madonna," April 18, 2012, https://www.youtube.com/watch?v=orwhstP7DIU.

9. Camille Paglia, "Madonna—Finally, a Real Feminist," *New York Times Magazine*, December 14, 1990.

10. Daily Mail Reporter, "Copycat Queen: Lady Gaga Steals More of Madonna's Iconic 80s Style in Her New Music Video Edge of Glory," *Daily Mail*, June 17, 2011, www .dailymail.co.uk/tvshowbiz/article-2004566/Lady-Gaga-steals-Madonnas-iconic-80s -style-new-music-video-Edge-Glory.html.

11. "Rihanna Wants to be a Madonna," *Metro News*, July 17, 2007, http://metro.co.uk /2007/07/17/rihanna-wants-to-be-a-madonna-534173.

12. WENN, "Stefani: 'I Didn't Copy Madonna,'" *Contactmusic.com*, November 3, 2005, http://hub.contactmusic.com/news-article/stefani-i-didnt-copy-madonna.

13. Rick Florino, "Feature: Artists on Madonna," *Artists Direct*, September 18, 2009, http://www.artistdirect.com/entertainment-news/article/feature-artists-on-madonna /6153129.

## Michelle Obama

1. "Michelle Obama and Laura Bush," *The View*, New York: ABC, aired June 18, 2008, accessed online on 3/22/2014, https://www.youtube.com/watch?v=aPJ8xpBYpJ0.

2. Alma Halbert Bond, *Michelle Obama: A Biography* (Santa Barbara: Greenwood, 2012), 51.

3. Kate Betts, *Everyday Icon: Michelle Obama and the Power of Style* (New York: Potter Style, 2011), 1.

4. Ibid., 13.

5. "Michelle Obama and Laura Bush," *The View*, June 18, 2008.

6. "Michelle Obama Workout Routine: First Lady Hits Gym Before Dawn—And Before Hubby," *Huffington Post*, August 21, 2012, http://www.huffingtonpost.com /2012/08/21/michelle-obama-workout-routine-fitness-exercise_n_1817879.html.

7. Betts, *Everyday Icon*, 10.

8. Ibid., 10.

9. "Michelle Obama and Laura Bush," *The View*, June 18, 2008.

10. Lisa Stark, "Reporter's Notebook: The Michelle Obama Effect," *ABC News*, http://abcnews.go.com/Politics/OTUS/reporters-notebook-michelle-obama-effect/story?id=17164394.

## Lady Gaga

1. "Lady Gaga—Born This Way." *YouTube*, 7:19, posted by "LadyGagaVEVO," February 27, 2011, https://www.youtube.com/watch?v=wV1FrqwZyKw.

2. Ibid.

3. Christine Kathleen, *Lady Gaga—Unabridged Guide*, (Dayboro, Australia: Emereo Publishing, 2012), 5.

4. "Lady Gaga CNN IBN TV India Interview 2011 (Hakim Boudi)," *YouTube*, 14:56, posted by "gagahakim's channel," February 19, 2011, https://www.youtube.com/watch?v=bJlr3ryHc34.

5. Elizabeth Goodman, *Lady Gaga: Critical Mass Fashion* (New York: St. Martin's Griffin, 2010), 140.

6. Bridget Heos, *Lady Gaga* Megastars (New York: Rosen Central, 2011), 10.

7. Maureen Callahan, *Poker Face: The Rise and Rise of Lady Gaga* (New York: Hyperion, 2010), 35.

8. Amber L. Davisson, *Lady Gaga and the Remaking of Celebrity Culture* (Jefferson, NC: McFarland & Company, 2013), 128.

9. Emily Herbert, *Lady Gaga: Behind the Fame* (New York: The Overlook Press, 2010), 98.

## Michelle Phan

1. Michelle Phan, "How to Build Confidence," *YouTube*, 5:26, July 13, 2014, https://www.youtube.com/watch?v=20p5o6QaQfg.

2. Michelle Phan, "Egg Mask Facial," *YouTube*, 5:52, June 12, 2009, https://www.youtube.com/watch?v=Rk4xdYt3ick.

3. Michelle Phan, *Make Up: Your Life Guide to Beauty, Style, and Success—Online and Off* (New York: Harmony Books, 2014), 4.

4. Ibid., 1.

5. Ibid., 5.

6. Ibid.

7. Ibid.

8. Ibid., 6.

9. Ibid.

10. Ibid., VIII.

11. Michelle Phan, "Airplane Beauty Tips," *YouTube*, 5:01, September 23, 2010, https://www.youtube.com/watch?v=wKop_8mlQ2s.

12. Phan, *Make Up*, 17.

13. Ibid., 16.

14. Ibid., 50.

15. Ibid., 112.

### Tavi Gevinson

1. Lizzie Widdicomb, "Tavi Says: Fashion Dictates from a Fourteen-Year-Old," *The New Yorker*, September 20, 2010, http://www.newyorker.com/magazine/2010/09/20/tavi-says#ixzz107y5klqY.

2. Tina Essmaker and Tammi Heneveld, "Tavi Gevinson, Actor/Editor/Writer," *The Great Discontent*, 1 (June 2014), http://thegreatdiscontent.com/interview/tavi-gevinson.

3. "Tavi Gevinson: Not So Afraid of Ambition," *CBS News*, August 31, 2014 http://www.cbsnews.com/news/tavi-gevinson-not-so-afraid-of-ambition.

4. "Tavi Gevinson Grows Up," *The New York Times/T Magazine* On Set, 3:02, June 6, 2014, http://www.nytimes.com/video/t-magazine/100000002898693/tavi-gevinson.html.

5. "I-Need-to-Clutter-My-Room-and-Make-Crowns Kind of Way," *XO Style Stalker*, August 14, 2014, http://www.xostylestalker.com/need-clutter-room-make-crowns-kind-way (page discontinued).

6. Amanda Fortini, "How Sassy Is Tavi Gevinson?" *The New York Times Magazine*, August 31, 2011, http://www.nytimes.com/2011/09/04/magazine/how-sassy-is-tavi-gevinson.html.

7. Tavi Gevinson, "Still Figuring It Out," *TEDxTeen*, 7:38, April 9, 2012. http://tedxteen.com/talks/tedxteen-2012/112-tavi-gevinson-still-figuring-it-out.

8. Essmaker and Heneveld, *The Great Discontent*, 191.

9. Krista Burton, "How to Look Like You Weren't Just Crying in Less Than Five Minutes," *Rookie* March 23, 2012, http://www.rookiemag.com/2012/03/how-to-look-like-you-werent-just-crying-in-less-than-five-minutes.

10. Tavi Gevinson, *Rookie Yearbook Two*, Montreal: Drawn & Quarterly, 2013, 56.

11. Tavi Gevinson, "Still Figuring It Out," *TEDxTeen*, April 9, 2012.

12. Christopher Zara, "'This Is Our Youth' Broadway Review: Michael Cera, Tavi Gevinson, and Kieran Culkin Don't Want to Grow Up," *Newsweek.com*, September 12, 2014, http://www.newsweek.com/our-youth-broadway-review-michael-cera-tavi -gevinson-and-kieran-culkin-dont-want-270095.

13. Hannah Ongley, "Tavi Gevinson's Guide to Life As Told by Her Reddit AMA: From the Perfect Pizza Slice to Dealing with Impostor Syndrome," *Stylelite*, September 18, 2014, http://www.styleite.com/news/tavi-gevinsons-guide-to-life-as-told-by-her-reddit -ama.

14. Ibid.

15. Abbey Goodman, "Tavi Gevinson May Take Over the World While You Read This," *CNN*, January 2, 2013, http://www.cnn.com/2013/01/02/showbiz/celebrity -news-gossip/tavi-gevinson-profile.

## The New Fashionista Hall of Fame

1. "Bethany Mota on How She Overcame Bullies and Became the Queen of YouTube!" *Seventeen Magazine*, slides 1–6, accessed July 23, 2014, www.seventeen.com /celebrity/g1183/bethany-mota-pictures.

2. "Beauty Blogger Bethany Mota on her New YouTube Show 'Make Me Over,'" *Teen Vogue*, accessed August 9, 2013, http://www.teenvogue.com/beauty/2012-08 /bethany-mota-macbarbie07-make-me-over?slide=4.

3. Hillary Beard, Serena Williams, and Venus Williams, *Venus & Serena: Serving from the Hip: Ten Rules for Living, Loving. and Winning* (Boston: Houghton Mifflin, 2005), 61.

4. "Where Did You Get that Dress?" *Northwestern.edu*, http://www.northwestern.edu /magazine/spring2011/campuslife/zoe_damacela_print.html.

5. Donahue, Wendy, "Remarkable Woman: Zoe Damacela," *Chicago Tribune*, June 29, 2012, http://articles.chicagotribune.com/2012-06-29/features/ct-tribu-remarkable -damacela-20120629_1_sewing-class-national-youth-entrepreneurship-challenge -clothing-business.

6. Jeré Longman, "Praising Griner Proves Far Easier Than Stopping Her," *New York Times*, March 19, 2013, http://womentalksports.com/headline/praising-griner-proves -far-easier-than-stopping-her (page discontinued).

7. "Brittney Griner," *My Ink*, season 1, episode 4, 4:39, AOL Originals, October 30, 2013, http://on.aol.com/show/517937510-my-ink/517990709.

# Selected Bibliography

Allgor, Catherine. *A Perfect Union: Dolley Madison and the Creation of the American Nation*. New York: Henry Holt, 2007.

Arnold, Janet. *Queen Elizabeth's Wardrobe Unlock'd: The Inventories of the Wardrobe of Robes Prepared in July 1600*. Oakville, CT: David Brown Book Co., 1988.

Badman, Keith, *Marilyn Monroe: The Final Years*. New York: Thomas Dunne Books/St. Martin's Press, 2012.

Baker, Jean-Claude and Chris Chase. *Josephine: The Hungry Heart*. New York: Cooper Square Press, 2001.

Betts, Kate. *Everyday Icon: Michelle Obama and the Power of Style*. New York: Potter Style, 2011.

Blumer, Ronald. "Dolley Madison." *American Experience*. Directed by Muffie Meyer. Arlington: PBS, 2010, DVD.

Bond, Alma H. *Michelle Obama: A Biography*. Santa Barbara, CA: Greenwood, 2012.

Callahan, Maureen. *Poker Face: The Rise and Rise of Lady Gaga*. New York: Hyperion, 2010.

Chan, B. Anthony. *Perpetually Cool: The Many Lives of Anna May Wong (1905–1961)*. Lanham, MD: Scarecrow Press, 2003.

DeGeneres, Ellen. *Seriously . . . I'm Kidding*. New York: Grand Central Publishing, 2011.

Druesedow, Jean and Kohle Yohannon. *Katharine Hepburn: Rebel Chic*. New York: Skira Rizzoli, 2012.

Essmaker, Tina and Tammi Heneveld. "Tavi Gevinson, Actor/ Editor/Writer," *The Great Discontent*. 1 (June 2014), thegreatdiscontent.com/interview/tavi-gevinson.

Gevinson, Tavi, ed. *Rookie Yearbook Two*. Montreal: Drawn & Quarterly, 2014.

Hellstern, Melissa. *How to Be Lovely: The Audrey Hepburn Way of Life*. New York: Dutton, 2005.

Hepburn, Katharine. *Me: Stories of My Life*. New York: Knopf, 1991.

Hodges, Graham. *Anna May Wong: From Laundryman's Daughter to Hollywood Legend*. Hong Kong: Hong Kong University Press, 2012.

Hong, Yunah. *Anna May Wong: In Her Own Words*. Directed by Yunah Hong, Eastwind Productions, New York, 2013, DVD.

Jules-Rosette, Bennetta. *Josephine Baker in Art and Life: The Icon and the Image.* Champaign, IL: University of Illinois Press, 2007.

Karbo, Karen. *The Gospel According to Coco Chanel: Life Lessons from the World's Most Elegant Woman.* Augusta, GA: Skirt!, 2009.

Karbo, Karen. *How to Hepburn: Lessons on Living from Kate the Great.* New York: Bloomsbury, 2007.

Kathleen, Christine, *Lady Gaga: Unabridged Guide.* Brisbane, Australia: Emereo Publishing, 2012.

Kettenmann, Andrea. *Frida Kahlo, 1907–1954: Pain and Passion.* Los Angeles: Taschen, 2007.

Maychick, Diana. *Audrey Hepburn: An Intimate Portrait.* New York: Citadel, 1996.

Morrison, John and Jamie Pietras. *Frida Kahlo* (The Great Hispanic Heritage). New York: Chelsea House Publishers, 2010.

Morton, Andrew. *Madonna.* New York: St. Martin's Press, 2002.

Nickens, Christopher and George Zeno. *Marilyn in Fashion: The Enduring Influence of Marilyn Monroe.* Philadelphia: Running Press, 2012.

Phan, Michelle. *Make Up: Your Life Guide to Beauty, Style, and Success—Online and Off.* New York: Harmony Books, 2014.

Preston, Diana. *Cleopatra and Antony: Power, Love, and Politics in the Ancient World.* New York: Walker & Company, 2009.

Roller, Duane W. *Cleopatra: A Biography.* New York: Oxford University Press, 2010.

Schiff, Stacy. *Cleopatra: A Life.* New York: Little, Brown and Company, 2010.

Schroeder, Alan and Heather Lehr Wagner. *Josephine Baker: Entertainer.* New York: Chelsea House Publishers, 2006.

Sherrow, Victoria. *Encyclopedia of Hair: A Cultural History.* Westport, CT: Greenwood Press, 2006.

Spoto, Donald. *Jacqueline Bouvier Kennedy Onassis: A Life*. New York: St. Martin's Press, 2000.

Stechler, Amy. *The Life and Times of Frida Kahlo*. Directed by Amy Stechler. Arlington: PBS, 2006. DVD.

Taraborrelli, J. Randy. *The Secret Life of Marilyn Monroe*. New York: Grand Central Publishing, 2009.

Weber, Caroline. *Queen of Fashion: What Marie Antoinette Wore to the Revolution*. New York: Picador/Henry Holt, 2007.

Weir, Alison. *The Life of Elizabeth I*. New York: Ballantine Books, 1998.

Wood, Ean. *The Josephine Baker Story*. London: Sanctuary Publishing, 2000.

Zweig, Stefan. *Marie Antoinette: The Portrait of an Average Woman*. New York: Grove Press, 2002.

# Fashion Dictionary

## Skirts & Dresses

**A-line skirt or dress**—A garment that is fitted at the waist and then flares out toward the bottom, giving the shape of a letter "A." The style originated with Christian Dior in his spring 1955 line.

**Baby doll dress**—An empire waist dress with a low, scooped neckline and a shortened hemline that hits above the knee.

**Bubble dress**—A dress with a tapered hemline that ends in a bubble shape.

**Bias cut**—Fabrics that are cut on the diagonal. This type of cut often gives a more flattering fit because the diagonal cut clings to curves better.

**Cheongsam**—A traditional Chinese gown made of embroidered fabric and a standup collar and a button closure on the right side of the neck. (Also called a Qipao.)

**Cinch waist**—A waist that is pulled in usually by a belt.

**Décolleté**—A low-cut neckline.

**Dropped waist**—A waistline that falls below the natural waist.

**Empire waist**—A waistline that starts under the bust. According to legend, Empress Josephine Bonaparte made the style popular to hide her pregnant belly.

**Jumper**—A loose-fitting sleeveless dress worn over a boatneck long-sleeved shirt.

**Midi skirt**—A dress or skirt with a hemline that falls at the widest point of the calf.

**Mini skirt**—A skirt four inches above the knee.

**Pencil skirt**—A skirt cut in one slim line from the hips to the hem.

**Sack dress**—A short, waistless, loose-fitting dress.

**Sheath dress**—A slim-fitting dress usually with a longer hemline.

**Shift dress**—A sleeveless, knee-length dress with a wide neckline, usually cut in an A-line.

**Shirt dress**—A knee-length dress with a shirt collar, usually worn belted at the waist.

**Wrap dress**—A one-piece, jersey dress with left and right panels that cross in the front and are tied together with a sash.

## Fabrics

**Brocade**—Often very luxurious, a heavy silk fabric that typically has a raised pattern with gold or silk thread. The technique to create a brocade fabric originated in Byzantium (today's Istanbul, Turkey) in the Middle Ages and spread throughout Europe. Marie Antoinette wore many dresses made of brocade fabric.

**Jersey**—A stretchy, knit fabric made from wool, silk, cotton, or rayon. Originally made of just wool, jersey originated in the Isle of Jersey off the English coast and was used to make sturdy clothing for fishermen.

**Silk**—A soft, strong fabric made from the fiber produced by silk worms. Silk production originated in China in prehistoric times.

## Hats, Jewelry, Shoes, Accessories

**Ballerina flats**—Soft, round-toed slippers with a thin heel.

**Choker**—A necklace that sits right at the throat.

**Cloche**—A close-fitting, bell-shaped hat popular in the 1920s.

**Clutch**—A small, usually strapless, handbag most often worn in the evening.

**Fishnets**—Stockings with a crisscross weave pattern.

**Gladiator sandals**—Flat, open-toed sandals with straps that wind up the leg, typically to the ankle or knee. Gladiator sandals were first worn by Roman soldiers in 35 CE.

**Kitten heel**—A shoe with a curvy, less than one-inch heel.

**Mules**—A backless shoe with a closed toe box. Mules are often hard to walk in because they slip off the foot easily. For this reason, they were usually worn by aristocrats in the eighteenth century who traveled by gilded carriage and not by their own two feet.

**Platforms**—Around for over two thousands years, platforms are shoes with a stacked sole made from cork, plastic, rubber, or wood.

**Stilettos**—A shoe with a thin heel that is usually two to three inches high. It is named after the stiletto dagger—a sharp, thin blade. Marilyn Monroe made these popular in the 1940s.

**Strappy sandals**—Shoes with straps across the toe box and usually the ankle too.

**T-strap shoes**—A shoe with two straps that form a T-shape—one that goes vertically up the foot and another that wraps around the ankle.

## Tops

**Cardigan**—A collarless sweater with buttons all the way down the front that can be worn open or closed. The cardigan got its name from England's Earl Cardigan, who wore a shoulder cape buttoned at the neck.

**Crop top**—A shirt that ends above the navel.

**Peasant shirt**—A loose-fitting blouse with loose-fitting sleeves cut usually into an empire waist.

**Peplum**—A top or dress that has a flounce that flares out from the waist.

## Pants & Shorts

**Bell-bottoms**—Pants that flare out into a bell shape at the bottom.

**Breeches**—Leggings that fasten below the knee and are usually worn when riding horses.

**Capri pants**—Close-fitting pants with a hemline a few inches below the knee.

**Cigarette pants**—Slim, tapered pants with a hemline right above the ankles.

**Leggings**—Thicker form-fitting pants that resemble tights.

**Tuxedo pants**—Black pants with a satin stripe that runs down the side of each leg.

## General Fashion Terms

**Embroidery**—Ornamentation of a fabric using decorative hand or machine stitches.

**Haute couture**—French for "high sewing," haute couture refers to the design houses that make exclusive fashions for women.

**High-low fashion**—Mixing high-end fashion and custom tailored pieces with more casual and affordable everyday pieces.

**Vintage**—The term is often used to describe any old clothing items, but it technically only applies to clothing that is between 20–100 years old.